Training Manual for Working with Older People in Residential and Day Care Settings

of related interest

Becoming a Trainer in Adult Abuse Work
A Practical Guide
Jacki Pritchard
ISBN 1 85302 913 0

Elder Abuse Work
Best Practice in Britain and Canada
Edited by Jacki Pritchard
ISBN 1 85302 704 9

Working with Elder Abuse
A Training Manual for Home Care, Residential and Day Care Staff
Jacki Pritchard
IBSN 1 85302 418 X

Male Victims of Elder Abuse
Their Experiences and Needs
Jacki Pritchard
ISBN 1 85302 999 8

Good Practice in Working with Victims of Violence
Edited by Hazel Kemshall and Jacki Pritchard
ISBN 1 85302 768 5
Good Practice in Social Work 8

Groupwork in Social Care
Planning and Setting up Groups
Julie Phillips
ISBN 1 85302 829 0

The Essential Groupworker
Teaching and Learning Creative Groupwork
Mark Doel and Catherine Sawdon
ISBN 1 85302 823 1

The Care Homes Legal Handbook
Jeremy Cooper
ISBN 1 85302 064 9

Good Practice in Counselling People Who Have Been Abused
Edited by Zetta Bear
ISBN 1 85302 424 4
Good Practice in Social Work 4

Counselling Adult Survivors of Child Sexual Abuse
Christine Sanderson
ISBN 1 85302 138 5

Training Manual for Working with Older People in Residential and Day Care Settings

Jacki Pritchard

Jessica Kingsley Publishers
London and New York

First published in the United Kingdom in 2003
by Jessica Kingsley Publishers Ltd
116 Pentonville Road
London N1 9JB, England
and
29 West 35th Street, 10th fl.
New York, NY 10001-2299, USA

www.jkp.com

Copyright © Jacki Pritchard 2003

Library of Congress Cataloging in Publication Data

Pritchard, Jacki.
    Training manual for working with older people in residential and day care settings / Jacki Pritchard.
        p. cm.
    Includes bibliographical references and index.
    ISBN 1-84310-123-8 (pbk. : alk. paper)
     1. Aged--Care--United States--Handbooks, manuals etc. 2. Caregivers--United States--Handbooks, manauls, etc. I. Title.

HV1461.P758 2003
362.6'1--dc21   2002043371

British Library Cataloguing in Publication Data

A CIP catalogue record for this book is available from the British Library

ISBN 1 84310 123 8

Printed and Bound in Great Britain by
Athenaeum Press, Gateshead, Tyne and Wear

*This book is dedicated to all the residential and day care staff
I have met and worked with over the years because
they have helped me to learn and experience.*

Contents

Key to symbols used in book

The following symbols have been used throughout the manual for ease of recognition:

case examples

role play

suggested videos

exercises

quiz sheets

handouts

case studies

All pages located at the end of chapters and marked ✓ may be photocopied for training pages, but may not be reproduced in other forms without the prior permission of the publisher.

Acknowledgements

First of all I am indebted to Luke Bond for being persistent in persuading me to work with him on producing a video on abuse; this was how it all started. The idea for writing the manual came after making several videos for the BVS series.

Many people have supported me in very practical ways while I was writing the manual. Janice Ward, Shaun Davidson and Olwen Williams have been totally invaluable. I would also like to thank Ann Stoner for giving me all the information I needed on NVQs.

There have been a number of people who have actively encouraged me throughout the summer months and kept me going – Amy Lankester-Owen, Lynne Hinchliff and Debi Jones.

Finally, I would also like to express my gratitude to the organisations which *did* respond to my request for information which could be included in the manual.

Glossary of Terms

Agency   A government office or department providing a particular service.

Care worker   A person who works in a home or day centre.

Day centre   Any day care establishment.

Home   This manual is aimed at all homes where care is provided, so the word 'home' may refer to a residential or nursing home, regardless of size.

Organisation   A body of people with a particular purpose.

Participant   A care worker who may be receiving training on a formal training course or on an 'in-house' basis. A person who is taking part in an exercise.

Service user   An older person living in a home or attending a day centre.

Trainer   Anyone who has a responsibility for training, e.g. manager, training officer, NVQ co-ordinator/assessor.

Chapter 1

Training Care Workers and Using the Manual

Training residential and day care staff

When I look back over the past 20 years in the field of social care, it has always seemed unfair to me that staff working in residential and day care settings have not regularly been offered the same quality training as other groups of workers. They were never given the same opportunities for their professional development. It was often argued that the cascade method of training was 'good enough'. Things have improved dramatically in recent years with the advent of National Vocational Qualifications (NVQs) and now the Induction and Foundation Standards which were introduced on 1 April 2002 by the National Training Organisation for Social Care (Training Organisation for the Personal Social Services 2001).

I have always believed that residential and day care workers, who are such vital people in providing support and care for service users, are very much undervalued. They have much more contact with service users than most professionals. Because of this, they get to know and understand service users on a much deeper level than a social worker who perhaps only sees the person for an hour at a time. The introduction of the NHS and Community Care Act 1990 changed social workers' way of working; traditional social work went out of the window when care management was introduced. Residential and day care workers are fundamental to the care management system — they can assess, monitor and review because they are care providers. Surely workers who are such a crucial part of the system should be offered thorough and in-depth training?

The growth in NVQ training has been enormous and does offer opportunities for personal and professional development to care workers. However, it has to be recognised that it is a huge and demanding commitment to undertake. I still get annoyed when agencies/organisations do not include care workers in mainstream training. It worries me that training departments/sections are often divided into specialisms and this results in certain groups of staff being discriminated against or being seen as low priority. I would like to illustrate a typical example I come across frequently. (I hope this is going to become less common in the future.)

An NVQ section might have been developed in a social services department and offers excellent support to staff, but when it comes to training on adult abuse staff like the home carers, residential and day care staff are rarely included in courses with social workers, health workers and the police. Previously they have been offered basic awareness training in their own staff groups or received cascade training. This is not good enough: care workers are front line workers who identify abuse. They need more than basic awareness training – they need to know about investigations, pre-senting information at case conferences: the topic list goes on! If multi-agency training is to be promoted, they should be able to mix with other professionals.

With the introduction of the Training Organisation for the Personal Social Services (TOPSS) Standards, care workers are going to be trained within very short time limits (which someone new to the field of social care might find quite daunting – as may the managers who have to train them!).

> Managers must ensure that all new staff complete the induction standards within the first six weeks of employment and the foundation standards within the first six months. They will need to be sure that there is a record of this available for use during inspections and that the staff themselves have their own record. (TOPSS 2001, p.6)

The TOPSS Standards are very comprehensive and give a sound framework from which good practice can be promoted. However, from a new care worker's point of view there is a lot of information to be assimilated in a short space of time; this could feel very overwhelming. It must be acknowledged that there is lot of overlap between the Standards; in some ways this is helpful because learning points will be reinforced. The purpose of this manual is to help develop the training which must be undertaken and to make it an enjoyable experience for care workers.

How the manual came into being

I decided to write this manual whilst I was working in conjunction with Luke Bond to produce a series of training videos which could be used to help care workers meet the new TOPSS Standards. The idea was to write a training manual which could be used in conjunction with the series of videos. That was the basic aim, but when planning the manual it became clear that it could also be used by care workers who are undertaking NVQs in Care or Promoting Independence. It should be emphasised that the manual can be used independently or in conjunction with the series of videos (see Appendix 1).

What the manual is and isn't

The main objective of the manual is to promote good practice in working with older people who live in a home or attend a day centre. It concentrates on looking at the main (but not all) subject areas which are required to meet the TOPSS Standards. I have divided the chapters into what I think are the most important subject areas from a practice point of view. The manual is *not* a guide to rules and regulations (for example, fire regulations, food hygiene etc.) although references will be made to such points. A manual like this cannot cover everything. The subjects covered are massive in themselves. I have tried to include guidance as to where managers, trainers and care workers can obtain good and useful information both for themselves and service users, so I hope the manual will not only be a good training tool but also a helpful resource for information sources.

Who can use the manual

All sorts of people could be given the remit to train care workers (e.g. managers, senior staff, training officers, NVQ co-ordinators) and the manual is obviously aimed at those people. Some of them might not feel confident about training their staff so I have tried to set out the manual in a way which highlights key training issues in order to meet the TOPSS Standards. Although the book is primarily a training manual, care workers (and anyone else who comes into contact with older people in homes or day centres, e.g. advocates, volunteers) will find some of the discussion useful to read in order to increase their own knowledge and understanding of older people.

Layout of the chapters

As already stated, there is considerable overlap between some of the TOPSS Standards. I have tried to divide the chapters into clear subject areas. The beginning of each chapter lists the TOPSS Standards to which the chapter relates, but I have also included the relevant units for NVQ candidates.

I felt whilst writing the manual that the issues which needed be covered within each chapter needed to be addressed in different ways. Consequently, the materials in each chapter vary – for example in some chapters there are numerous case studies, in others there are none, but lots of case examples. A wide range of materials are included in the chapters:

- discussion of the subject
- case examples
- role play
- suggested reading
- useful organisations/websites
- videos
- exercises
- quiz sheets
- handouts
- case studies.

For ease the exercises, quiz sheets, handouts, and case studies sheets have been located at the end of each chapter. The reader is alerted to the appropriate handout or case study by the appropriate symbol within the body of the text.

There is often much confusion about terminology and jargon. I always find it useful to check on meanings in a dictionary so I have included some **Dictionary Definitions** which can be used to stimulate some discussion. All the definitions have been taken from the *Compact Oxford English Dictionary* (2000). I have also inserted **Good Practice Points**, **Key Questions** and **Tasks**, which the trainer can utilise in different ways.

Equipment needed

Managers within homes or day centres may not always think about what equipment might be needed for a training session. The exercises included in this manual will require:

- video/TV presenter
- flipchart stand
- flipchart paper
- flipchart pens/markers
- pads of A4 paper
- pens
- Post-It stickers
- Blu-Tack
- cardboard box.

Additionally, managers may wish to supply their care workers with:

- folders for handouts
- A4 lever arch files for notes.

Using the training materials

The training of care workers is likely to take place in a variety of ways at different times; that is:

- on the job
- supervision sessions
- staff meetings
- induction week
- formal courses (in-house or externally provided).

It is important for any trainer to make training interesting and not a chore for the care workers. Introducing a variety of training methods is essential to maintain interest and for learning, so different materials have been incorporated into each chapter.

Exercises

The exercises which are included can be adapted to suit the needs of the training situation. I was very conscious when writing the manual of the fact that some care workers might meet with a manager in small groups to train whereas others will be trained in larger groups on formal training courses (for example, 16–20 participants). Consequently, I was careful to develop the exercises so that they could be adapted to suit the size of the group. Also, managers may choose to adapt some exercises to be used in supervision sessions on a one-to-one basis. A lot of the exercises will be related to the care worker having to think about themselves and then relate the learning points to service users. Service users should not be seen as 'different'.

Each exercise gives guidance about:

- **Objective** – what the exercise aims to achieve.

- **Participants** – how they should work; that is, individually, in pairs or small groups (i.e. 4–5 participants).

- **Equipment** – which the trainer may need to prepare beforehand (see below).

- **Time** – this is a rough guide to how long the work will take the participants; it does *not* include time for feedback. The trainer should decide the duration of feedback depending on the agenda for the course, and should always make it clear to the participants how long will be given.

- **Task** – what the trainer will ask the participants to do.

- **Feedback** – the trainer should explain what is expected from participants in feedback and time should be left for open discussion to ensure that the objective of the exercise has been achieved.

- **Note for trainer** – in some exercises there is additional guidance for the trainer.

Case examples and case studies

Case examples are used in the text to illustrate points in the discussion. Some trainers may wish to use them in a similar way in training sessions. The case studies have a different objective; they should be used to facilitate participation and can be used to check out whether care workers have understood the subject matter under consideration. They can be used either for study in small groups or be given to a care worker to work on in between training or supervision sessions.

Quiz sheets

Quiz sheets have been included to test out a care worker's current state of knowledge – to identify gaps or where they are mistaken about something. The quiz sheets should *not* be seen as a 'test'. It is hoped they can be utilised in an enjoyable way!

Role play

As a trainer I know everyone hates role play. It *can* be a useful way to rehearse and learn, but only if it is done in a safe environment. Trainers should be honest about role play and not cover it up in terms like 'simulation'. Participants need reassurance that they can learn by their mistakes. I think it is pointless doing role play if people are terrified and I do not think anyone should be made to do something which is not necessary. I propose that role play should be done in a certain way, explained in Handout 1.1. Participants are not watched by anyone else (so they feel safe) and they can stop and start the role play, so they learn by their botch-ups! The trainer should decide how long the role play should run for; I think ten minutes can be a good starting point until participants feel more confident. I have had very positive feedback about doing role play in this way.

Using the manual in conjunction with the videos

At the end of each chapter there is a section entitled **Videos** which lists the BVS videos which may be relevant to the subject of the chapter and can be incorporated into the training session (whatever form it is taking). The trainer should become familiar with a video before using it in training. This is because the videos can be used in a variety of ways. Some trainers may choose to show the video from start to finish at some point during the training session; others may choose to show parts of a video at different points in the session – perhaps when introducing one aspect of the topic under consideration or between exercises. At the end of each chapter I have indicated the main video(s) which can be used for the particular subject under consideration. I have also listed related videos which will aid further learning.

References and suggested reading lists

Sources which are mentioned in the text are referenced at the end of the manual. The **Suggested reading** section at the end of each chapter is primarily for care workers. The suggestions have been kept to a minimum, because I know that care workers have little time to read. So I have included in the section what I consider to be the most relevant and useful reading material related to the subject of the chapter. Trainers may want to refer more to the references section in order to read around more texts in preparation for training sessions.

Useful organisations

In Appendix 2 I have listed organisations that could be useful sources of information for care workers with the contact address, telephone/fax numbers, e-mail addresses and website (when available). At the end of each chapter there is a section entitled **Useful organisations** or **Useful information/websites** where I have named specific organisations which are particularly good because of their information leaflets or publications lists, which relate to what has been discussed in the chapter. I have read the information myself and only make recommendations where I think it would be worthwhile for care workers to take the time to contact these organisations. I am acutely aware that time is precious.

GUIDE TO DOING THE ROLE PLAYS

1. Don't be frightened – the role plays will be done in a safe environment – no one will watch you.

2. You will be given a role – you have ( ) minutes to think about the information you have been given on the sheet.

3. The role play will run for ( ) minutes.

4. If you botch up – say something wrong, get the giggles or whatever – stop the role play, discuss what happened with your partner(s) and restart from where you left off.

5. At the end, you will have ( ) minutes to debrief with your partner(s).

6. General feedback will be taken in a large group. Think about what you learnt from doing the role play.

Chapter 2
Principles of Care

Someone working in the field of social care might describe themselves as a 'caring person', but what does caring mean exactly?

Dictionary Definition

Care

The provision of what is necessary for the welfare and protection of someone or something.

Individuals show that they care in their own way; they will all do this differently. Some can express themselves easily verbally, others will demonstrate how they feel by their actions. In a professional role it is important that workers who are caring for service users are consistent in their practice and act within professional boundaries. This is why it is important that care workers understand the principles of care and give thought to how they can develop their practice to a high standard.

TOPSS Induction Standard 1 states that care workers should 'understand the importance of promoting the following values at all times:

- individuality and identity
- rights
- choice
- privacy
- independence
- dignity
- respect
- partnership.' (TOPSS 2001, p.14)

In addition there has to be an understanding of prejudice and equal opportunities. These subject areas will be the focus of this particular chapter. Other subjects which are included in Induction Standard 1 (worker relationships and communication) will be covered in the following chapters. First, let us consider what is meant by the term 'principle'.

What is a principle?

Managers and trainers need to be very careful about the terminology that they use when inducting or training care workers. Lots of words they use may be familiar to them but someone who is new to the social care field may be unsure of the jargon being used (and maybe too scared or embarrassed to ask if they do not understand!). Words are used interchangeably which can be very confusing for a worker; a good example is the subject of this chapter – 'principles' and 'values'. Words can also be interpreted differently depending on the context they are used in. Work may need to be undertaken with care workers about the use of words and terminology; exercises are included in the manual to address this issue. Trainers should be sensitive to the fact that some care workers may be lacking in confidence and feel threatened if they are put on the spot. So what are principles and values?

Dictionary Definitions

Principle

A fundamental truth or proposition serving as the foundation for belief or action; a rule or belief governing one's personal behaviour; morally correct behaviour and attitudes; a fundamental source or basis of something.

Value

The regard that something is held to deserve; importance or worth.

Values

Principles or standards of behaviour.

Discussing such terms can be difficult for care workers if it is not done in an interesting way. It is important for a trainer to relate the discussion to practice. Exercise 2.1 is an introductory exercise which can be a way of getting workers to think about what a good care worker should be doing.

History behind the principles

In 1989 the Department of Health produced *Homes Are For Living In*, which was a model for evaluating the quality of care provided, and quality of life experienced, in residential care homes for older people. The intention was that the model, which was 'devised for managers and inspectors as an aid to inspection, would also be suitable for use by residential care staff as a focus for self-evaluation and development, and by agencies charged with training those members of staff' (Department of Health 1989, p.6). Six basic values were identified to contribute to good quality care and life experience in homes:

- privacy
- dignity
- independence
- choice
- rights
- fulfilment.

Handout 2.1, p.54

Even though this model was developed over a decade ago, it is still very useful. The values from the model underpinned the NHS and Community Care Act 1990 and are now related to the principles of care which will now be considered in more detail.

Individuality and identity

It can be hard when working with a large group of people to remember that every service user has the right to be treated as an individual. Many people see older people as all the same, but in fact they are just like younger people – each different in their own way. Many homes and day centres are understaffed and consequently care workers can be under a great deal of pressure to get basic tasks done. It is bad practice to treat everyone as though they are the same yet some people do work in this way because it makes life easier; that is, time does not have to be spent getting to know someone and their preferences. Individuality must be respected; in order to do this care workers must think about the issue of identity. Identity is not just about physical appearance but about background (roots), history, how one behaves and lives their life. Everyone has their own identity because of 'who' they are; this identity will have developed from their genetic make up and influences by family/peer groups, society, culture, religion and life experience. Exercise 2.2 will help care workers to think about what makes service users different.

Many of the points which are about to be highlighted to promote good practice in caring cross over the six values mentioned above. The intention is to consider each principle but some are very closely linked together; for example, privacy and dignity. In order to maintain these values service users must be offered choice. The objective throughout is that service users must be treated as individuals and equally. So mention must be made of equal opportunities.

Equal opportunities

All care workers should read their organisation's equal opportunities policy and understand what it is trying to achieve. Many such policies are written in a jargonistic manner, so workers may need some explanation about *how* it relates to their practice. This will involve employing exercises on anti-oppressive and anti-discriminatory practice on which there are many texts available. Exercise 2.3 may be used as a starting point. Care workers need to remember that they should be doing things *with* service users rather than *to* them. Care workers should be mindful of equal opportunities and working in partnership with residents.

Good Practice Point

Care workers should be doing things **with** service users rather than **to** them.

Everyone has prejudices, even though they may not admit it.

Dictionary Definition

Prejudice
Preconceived opinion that is not based on reason or experience; unjust behaviour formed on such a basis.

Care workers will meet service users who are prejudiced and may have to intervene. Exercise 2.4 will help them to pre-empt some situations which may arise in the future.

It is crucial to promote equal opportunities by:

- treating service users as individuals

- not stereotyping or labelling service users

- respecting the rights of service users

- valuing the contribution service users can make to the home/day centre

- empowering service users.

Handout 2.4, p.57

Older people are often discriminated against because they do not have equal access to certain services. Once they reach the age of 65 certain services may become unavailable to them. Care workers should become familiar with the new *National Service Framework for Older People* (DH 2001b), the first standard of which is 'Rooting Out Age Discrimination' (see Chapter 4).

Handout 2.2, p.55

Privacy

> ### Dictionary Definition
>
> **Privacy**
> A state in which one is not observed or disturbed by others.

> ### Homes Are For Living In
>
> **Privacy**
> The right of individuals to be left alone or undisturbed and free from intrusion or public attention into their affairs. (Department of Health 1989)

The *National Minimum Standards* suggests that *Homes Are For Living In* should be referred to and states:

> The principles on which the home's philosophy of care is based must be ones which ensure that residents are treated with respect, that their dignity is preserved at all times, and that their right to privacy is always observed. (DH 2002, p.7)

Some people like to be surrounded by people most of the time. This may be because they grew up in a large family and it seems 'normal' not to have much time or space to oneself. Care workers should constantly remind themselves that living in a care home is not 'normal'. No matter how much effort is put into making a home 'homely' many of them will be large institutions – maybe with 40 or more service users. Care staff may get used to the environment they work in and easily forget that for new service users it may be difficult to make the adjustment. It may not be possible to have the same amount of privacy which was previously available at home. It may be particularly difficult for a person who has been living alone and is used to pleasing themselves about when, where and how they do things.

Privacy is about giving service users personal space and the opportunity to do things in private. The principle of privacy also needs to be linked to confidentiality. Service users need to be assured that they can live their lives without other service users having to know their business.

It is equally important for day care staff to think about maintaining privacy. Some day centres may be quite small and it might be that everyone can hear what is being said. Service users should be able to speak to workers in private, and workers should make the effort to ensure that service users feel they can ask for that opportunity without other service users knowing this.

Exercise 2.5 should help care workers to think about how they can maintain privacy.

✍ Case study 2.1, p.62

Case Example

Edwina had started to have a continence problem, which she was very embarrassed about. She was having to keep a record of how much urine she was passing for the continence nurse. She wanted to tell the day care workers about this, but did not want anyone else to know about the problem. She did talk in private to one of the workers, but when she came back in the lounge other service users started asking why she had needed to go into another room. The care worker was very good at intervening by suggesting they start a new activity which took the pressure of questions off Edwina.

Dignity

Dictionary Definition

Dignity
The state or quality of being worthy of respect; a composed or serious manner; a sense of pride in oneself.

Homes Are For Living In

Dignity
A recognition of the intrinsic value of people regardless of circumstances by respecting their uniqueness and their personal needs; treating with respect. (Department of Health 1989)

A point that will be reiterated throughout this manual is that care workers must get to know their service users. This will take time because trust has to be established. Not everyone is going to want to tell their life story or disclose what is bothering them to a complete stranger. However, a care worker should strive to find out what is important to a service user and to try to make them feel as comfortable as possible. One of the first things to consider is a very simple thing – what does the service user want to be called?

Names are important to everyone because they are very personal. Even if you hate your name it still belongs to you! How you refer to someone is a sign of respect. A care worker should never assume that it is alright to use someone's first name without asking permission to do so. Neither should a care worker readily accept what someone (e.g. a relative or member of staff) says about the use of nicknames or shortened names. A nickname can stay with a person for years and the truth can be that they hate it. There is also a tendency for people to shorten names, which can be very annoying if you happen to like the longer version.

Case Example

Daughter: My Mum has always been known as Nel. Her real name is Penelope, but nobody has ever used it.

Penelope: Actually I like the name Penelope. My father always used it.

Naming systems can be very different within other cultures. The British use of Mr, Mrs, Miss or Ms is not always appropriate. Service users from different ethnic groups may have several names (personal, family, religious names) and it may not be clear to a care worker which is which. There are useful sources which explain the use of names (Alibhai-Brown 1998; Henley and Schott 1999). A care worker should ask a service user about their name and not be afraid to admit their own lack of knowledge. The service user will probably be pleased that someone is showing an interest. Nor is there anything wrong with asking how to pronounce a name correctly. The example below shows how mistakes can be made regarding Welsh names.

Case Example

The following Welsh names are common ones that people have trouble with.

Male names

- Dafydd (pronounce Davith)
- Guto (pronounce Gito)
- Rheinallt (pronounce Rhay nallt – double l as in Llandudno)
- Rhodri (pronounce Rhodree)
- Urien (pronounce Irrien)

Female names

- Angharad (pronounce Ang harr ad)
- Llio (pronounce Llee o – double l as in Llandudno)
- Ilid (pronounce Ill id)
- Eluned (pronounce El in ed)

Surnames

- Llwyd (pronounce Ll oo id – double l as in Llandudno)
- Prydderch (pronounce Prer there ch [ch back of your throat])
- Gruffydd (pronounce Griffith)

An objective for a care worker is to maintain the dignity of a service user by treating them as adults. It is not uncommon to hear a care worker talking to a service user as though they are a child; this is known as infantilisation. A care worker may use words or phrases which they would use to their own children (e.g. 'now be a good girl'; 'behave yourself'). If someone is confused, a care worker may speak louder than normal even though the person is not deaf.

One of the worst fears for anyone can be their appearance and how they look to other people. An older person who becomes disabled in some way may feel very undignified when they have to wear some aid (e.g. continence pad, hearing aid) or they cannot do things for themselves anymore (e.g. they need help with going to the toilet or being bathed; they can no longer cut their own toe nails; they lose control of their bladder).

Exercise 2.6 will help care workers to think about what dignity means to themselves as well as to service users.

𝒢𝒶 Case studies 2.2 and 2.3, pp.63–4

It is important to find out what is important to a service user, so that they can maintain their appearance and dignity. It has already been said that care workers should give consideration to gender differences when thinking about all the principles of care, but this is particularly pertinent when considering issues surrounding privacy and dignity. A service user may not want to receive personal care or discuss certain matters with a worker from the opposite gender. In some cultures a male would not expect to discuss certain things with a female, e.g. financial matters.

Independence

Dictionary Definitions

Independence
The fact or state of being independent.

Independent
Free from outside control or influence.

Homes Are For Living In

Independence
Opportunities to think and act without reference to another person including a willingness to incur a degree of calculated risk. (Department of Health 1989)

Many older people will be entering a home or attending a day centre because they can no longer be fully independent. They may have to rely on people around them for some practical and emotional support. A care worker should encourage the service user to maintain as much independence as possible. The principle of independence is very much related to the principle of choice.

Care staff need to be careful not to be overprotective towards service users. Unfortunately, we are living in an era when workers in social care are having to cover their own backs. It is required that workers explain and justify all their actions. At a time when litigation is on the increase workers can become very wary about how they practise when they are encouraged to promote risk-taking. Consequently, there has been a massive increase in the importance of undertaking risk assessments (see Chapter 6).

When encouraging independence there will be elements of risk-taking activity. Care workers need to assess what a service user is capable of doing for themselves and ascertain their wishes as to how they wish to live their life; that is, promoting the concept of self-determination. For service users who are disabled in some way (either physically or mentally) the care worker's task is to empower.

It is all too easy for a care worker to do things *for* a service user rather than *with* them. Sometimes because the care worker is under pressure, s/he will intervene rather than letting the service user take their time. Doing simple tasks may mean a lot to a service user; for example, making a cup of tea. Simple examples of when a care worker might take over instead of trying to encourage the service user to do something for themselves are:

- serves meals/clears plates
- makes/pours drinks
- tidies up in the bedroom
- chooses clothes to wear
- administers medication
- does all the washing – when a woman might like to do her 'smalls' herself.

Exercise 2.7 is designed to get care workers to think of ways in which they can actively promote independence.

In some homes, not enough time is spent explaining to a service user that they are free to come and go as they please. Service users are sometimes under the misapprehension that they cannot leave the building. They should in fact be encouraged to maintain interests outside of the home; for example:

- sitting outside in the grounds

- shopping

- walking

- visiting friends/family

- attending church/mosque

- going to the pub

- using the local library.

Even if people are dependent in some way, there will be small tasks that they can still achieve. Undertaking such tasks with a care worker will give them some self-worth.

Case Example

Jane had been a keen gardener all her life, but now she was quite frail and said she felt 'like I have no energy at all'. The GP said he believed Jane was depressed and she needed some interest. Her keyworker suggested to Jane that she might be able to make up some window boxes for the home. Jane got quite enthused by the idea, so she made a list of the things she needed. The keyworker went to the local garden centre and got the things Jane had written down. Jane started making up the boxes and then maintained them through the year.

Homes and day centres should ensure that they are providing the correct equipment so that service users can maintain some independence; for example, hand/grab rails, slip mats for the bath. Service users need to feel safe.

Case Example

Tom had developed diabetes when he was in his 60s. Over the years he lost his sight and his left leg was amputated. His wife had cared for him until she died; she had been very protective of Tom and had not allowed him to do things for himself. When he was admitted to care he was surprised when staff gave him options and suggested he do things for himself. He also felt very frightened as it seemed he had to learn how to do things all over again. His wife had not encouraged him to use his prosthesis and used to push him round in a wheelchair. His keyworker arranged for Tom to be measured for a new prosthesis and obtained a walking stick, after which she regularly took time to guide Tom round the home, so that eventually he could find his way round independently.

Case study 2.4, p.65

Choice

Dictionary Definition

Choice
An act of choosing; the right or ability to choose.

Homes Are For Living In

Choice
Opportunity to select independently from a range of options. (Department of Health 1989)

No matter how hard a manager and staff try, it is impossible to get away from the fact that a home or day centre is an institution – a word which creates a very negative image. Some older people associate a home with the workhouse. There have to be some rules and regulations because a group of people are living and working together. For example, smoking has to be restricted to certain areas. Choice about how a service user wishes to live their life should be offered to service users, but it has to be acknowledged that there may be limitations because everyone living in the home or attending the day centre has to be considered. In some situations there will have to be a degree of compromise.

However, the starting point should be finding out from the service user how they would like to live their life once they are in the home or at day centre. They need to be able to maintain some control over their lives and have a sense of freedom.

NATIONAL MINIMUM STANDARDS

Standard 12

12.1 The routines of daily living and activities made available are flexible and varied to suit service users' expectations, preferences and capacities.

12.2 Service users have the opportunity to exercise their choice in relation to:

- leisure and social activities and cultural interests
- food, meals and mealtimes
- routines of daily living
- personal and social relationships
- religious observance. (Department of Health 2002, p.16)

Standard 14

14.1 The registered person conducts the home so as to maximise service users' capacity to exercise personal autonomy and choice. (Department of Health 2002, p.17)

For day centre users, staff will be offering choices about activities, participation and interaction with other service users.

Case Example

Lena was 74 years old and had become really interested in using a computer. She had attended a 'Computers for Beginners' course at the local community centre, but felt frustrated that she could not afford to buy a computer to have at home. She attended a local authority day centre twice a week – one day being Sunday. Lena was not really interested in the activities that were usually offered as they 'don't stretch my mind', so the day care staff offered Lena an alternative – it was suggested that she could use one of the computers in the home where the day centre was located. This computer was for the use of service users and did not contain any confidential files or information. Lena had a regular time booked when she could use the computer to practise her skills.

Exercise 2.8 will encourage care workers to evaluate whether they are giving service users enough choices.

Case studies 2.5 and 2.6, pp.66–7

Rights

Dictionary Definition

Right
A moral or legal entitlement to have or do something.

> **Homes Are For Living In**
>
> **Rights**
>
> The maintenance of all entitlements associated with citizenship. (Department of Health 1989)

It is important that all care workers become familiar with the Human Rights Act 1998 which brought the European Convention on Human Rights into the United Kingdom in October 2000 (Home Office 2001a and 2001b); see website www.homeoffice.gov.uk/hract.

Handout 2.6, p.59

Every human being has rights and a service user has the same rights as anyone living in the community. On admission to a home it is vital that time is taken to explain to the service user his/her rights and responsibilities. This should be clearly written within a contract.

NATIONAL MINIMUM STANDARDS

17.1   Service users have their legal rights protected, are enabled to exercise their legal rights directly and participate in the civic process if they wish. (Department of Health 2002, p.20)

Some typical examples which may concern a resident are the rights to:

- privacy
- safety
- health care
- information
- education
- expression/freedom of speech
- equality
- confidentiality.

The organisation should have in place a formal complaints procedure and this should be explained in detail. Most organisations will have a leaflet about this. This information and any related forms should be available in other languages, braille and large print.

NATIONAL MINIMUM STANDARDS

16.1 The registered person ensures that there is a simple, clear and accessible complaints procedure which includes the stages and timescales for the process, and that complaints are dealt with promptly and effectively.

16.2 The registered person ensures that the home has a complaints procedure which specifies how complaints may be made and who will deal with them, with an assurance that they will be responded to within a maximum of 28 days. (Department of Health 2002, p.20)

Case Example

Sylvia was 96 years old, she was physically frail but mentally sound. She had no living relatives, but a volunteer who had visited her when she lived in the community continued to visit her once a month. Sylvia had always been interested in politics and was a member of the Labour Party. In May she wanted to vote in the local elections and wanted someone to take her to the polling station. Staff said they did not have time to do this. Sylvia completed a complaints form about this and mentioned other things she was not happy about. Nothing happened and when Sylvia asked what the management were doing about her complaint she was told to 'wait and see'. Next time the volunteer visited Sylvia told her about the complaint and lack of response. The volunteer, who was also a trained advocate, offered to support Sylvia in pursuing her right to complain.

On admission, it is also important to explain about **confidentiality**, the sharing of information and access to files. Very few service users will take in all this information when they are probably very nervous about coming into care permanently. Therefore, it is imperative that staff keep going over these topics until they are sure that the service user understands. The word 'confidentiality' is often bandied about but many service users still do not really understand that confidentiality between a service user and a care worker is very different to keeping a confidence between two friends. Care workers cannot keep secrets.

Dictionary Definition
Confidential Intended to be kept secret; entrusted with private information.

A care worker needs to explain to a service user that confidentiality will be maintained wherever possible, but:

- any information given to a care worker belongs to the agency/organisation *not* to the individual worker

- a worker will share information with the line manager

- in some circumstances confidentiality may have to be broken.

Handout 2.7, p.60

The issue of confidentiality is discussed further in Chapter 8 and Exercise 8.2 can be used when training on principles of care.

Case Study 2.7 and Quiz Sheet 2.1 can be used to develop care workers' thinking in regard to rights.

Fulfilment

Dictionary Definition

Fulfilment

Satisfaction or happiness as a result of fully developing one's abilities or character.

Homes Are For Living In

Fulfilment

the realisation of personal aspirations and abilities in all aspects of daily life. (Department of Health 1989)

Coming to live in a home should not be seen as the end of the road. Many older people do see themselves as a burden and believe there is nothing to look forward to: 'I'm just living out my days here.' Care workers should be working with service users to encourage them to plan for the future. People are living longer so it is important that they live their lives to the full and strive to achieve any unfulfilled ambitions. Day centre staff can also support service users to achieve things. Care workers need to give some thought to how they can encourage service users to express their hopes and wishes regarding the future; they may refer to these wishes as dreams or fantasies – some of which may be achievable. For some people it is not easy to verbalise secret dreams or wishes – maybe because of the fear of being laughed at. Exercise 2.9 will help care workers think about how to express ambition.

Sometimes a service user knows that s/he is coming to the end of their life, and there may be certain things they need to do, but may need help with:

- Visit the house where s/he lived when they were first married.

- See the seaside just one more time.

- Hear the whole of the Bible/Koran read to them by the time they die.

- Write a letter to a relative to explain how they feel about an argument they had 30 years ago.

Case study 2.8, p.69

A service user's ambitions may be very simple – they may want to:

- walk to the toilet alone

- dress themselves

- cut their own toenails

- lose a certain amount of weight

- stop smoking.

In order to achieve hopes and ambitions service users may need from care workers:

- support – practical and emotional

- stimulation

- encouragement

- reassurance

- help in getting outside services.

Key Question

Is a service user being fulfilled or deskilled?

ᕬ Case study 2.9, p.70

In order to promote all the principles of care, a care worker should:

- get to know the service user

- build up trust

- learn about the service user's past life

- gain understanding about a service user's previous lifestyle

- encourage a service user to express their opinion/beliefs

- find out what and who is important to a service user

- have a flexible and creative approach.

Handout 2.8, p.61

Suggested reading

Alibhai-Brown, Y. (1998) *Caring for Ethnic Minority Elders.* London: Age Concern England.

Department of Health (1989) *Homes Are For Living In.* London: HMSO.

Henley, A. and Schott, J. (1999) *Culture, Religion and Patient Care in a Multi-Ethnic Society.* London: Age Concern England.

Home Office (2001a) *Human Rights Act: An Introduction.* London: Home Office Communication Directorate.

Useful information

National Service Framework for Older People information pack available from Department of Health, PO Box 777, London SE1 6XH or on the website www.doh.gov.uk/nsf/olderpeople.htm

Human Rights Unit Helpdesk, Home Office, 50 Queen Anne's Gate, London SW1H 9AT; www.homeoffice.gov.uk/hract

▣ VIDEOS

Principles of Care

Two other videos (which relate to the subject matter of the next two chapters) will also help care workers to understand the principles of care:

Role of the Care Worker

Needs of the Service User

WHAT DOES CARING FOR SOMEONE MEAN?

Objective

To focus on the word 'caring' and to relate it to work practices.

Participants

Individual work; then small group work.

Equipment

Paper and pens.
Flipchart paper and pens.

Time

10 minutes for individual work; 20 minutes for group work.

Task

Individual work

1. Make a list of situations when you have cared for someone else in your personal life.

2. Make brief notes about how you showed them you cared.

3. What do you do for a service user which could be considered to be 'caring'?

4. Are there any differences between caring for someone you know on a personal level and caring for someone in a work role?

Group work

Discuss Questions 1 to 4 as a group and make a list of key points.

Feedback

1. Each group will feed back their key points.

2. Trainer will encourage discussion about how care workers can show they care within professional boundaries.

WHAT MAKES A PERSON DIFFERENT?

Objective

To help care workers think about differences and identity.

Participants

Small groups.

Equipment

Flipchart paper and pens.

Time

20 minutes.

Task

1. Think about members of your family and friends. What makes you and them different?

2. Think of all the service users you currently work with. What makes you and them different?

3. What else makes people different?

Feedback

1. Groups feed back their list of differences.

2. Open discussion.

Note for trainer

The trainer should ensure that certain points are introduced to the open discussion if they are not introduced in feedback, i.e. likes/dislikes, life experience, hobbies/interests, backgrounds, age, gender, race, culture, religion, disability, sexuality etc.

PREJUDICE AND TREATING PEOPLE THE SAME

Objective

To get care workers to admit when they have been prejudiced towards someone.

Participants

Work in pairs.

Equipment

Paper and pens.

Time

15 minutes.

Task

1. Discuss with your partner people you do not like (this can be at work or in your personal life) and why you do not like them.

2. Ask your partner if s/he thinks you are being prejudiced.

3. Think of times in your life when you have treated someone differently; that is, you did not treat them in the same way as you would have done someone else in the same situation. Why was this?

Feedback

Trainer asks the large group to openly discuss times when they have been prejudiced and the reasons for their behaviour.

Note for trainer

This exercise needs to be done in a safe environment otherwise participants will not discuss this issue openly and honestly. Some ground rules need to be set emphasising confidentiality.

WHAT WOULD YOU DO IF?

Objective

To help care workers anticipate what they would do if they had to deal with a situation where a service user or staff member was being prejudiced or discriminatory.

Participants

Small groups.

Equipment

Photocopies of Handout 2.3.
Flipchart paper and pens.

Time

25 minutes.

Task

Discuss each scenario in turn. Write down ideas about what you would do in that situation.

Feedback

1. Trainer takes feedback on each scenario and encourages comments on the responses and further suggestions on how to handle the situations.

2. Open discussion.

WHEN MIGHT A SERVICE USER NEED PRIVACY?

Objective

To make care workers more aware about intruding on privacy.

Participants

Small groups.

Equipment

Flipchart paper and pens.
Copies of Handout 2.5 if required.

Time

20 minutes.

Task

1. Discuss and list situations when you feel you have intruded on a service user's privacy.

2. Discuss ways in which you could have avoided the intrusion and maintained privacy.

3. How could privacy be improved in your work setting?

Feedback

1. Groups highlight when bad practice has taken place in regard to privacy.

2. Open discussion about whether privacy is maintained in the participants' work settings.

3. Handout 2.5 can be used to further discussion.

DIGNITY

Objective

To think about when people may feel undignified.

Participants

Work in pairs.

Equipment

Paper and pens.

Time

20 minutes.

Task

1. Think of an occasion in your lifetime when you have felt undignified (examples could be: having to wear gym shorts; giving birth; having an internal examination).

2. Talk to a partner about how it felt at the time.

3. How do you feel talking about it now?

4. Think about situations when a service user in your home/day centre might feel undignified. Make a list.

Feedback

1. Participants put their lists up on the wall.

2. Participants read the lists.

3. Open discussion.

MAINTAINING INDEPENDENCE

Objective

To think about ways in which even the most dependent people can maintain some degree of independence.

Participants

Groups of 3.

Equipment

Flipchart paper and pens.

Time

30 minutes.

Task

1. Each worker thinks of one service user who is heavily dependent because of either physical or mental disability.

2. Discuss ways you could help the three service users to maintain some independence.

3. For each service user list the objective followed by a strategy (i.e. specific things which could be done to help).

Feedback

1. Each trio presents their strategies.

2. Open discussion.

GIVING CHOICES

Objective

For care workers to evaluate whether they are giving service users enough choices.

Participants

Small groups.

Equipment

Flipchart paper and pens.

Time

20 minutes.

Task

1. Make a list of choices you give service users on a day to day basis.

2. Are there things you would like to offer service users but you cannot do so currently? Why is this?

3. Do you ever deliberately not give a service user a choice? Why is this?

Feedback

1. Groups present their choices.

2. Open discussion about whether real choices are given or if they are restricted by staff/management/organisation.

3. Discussion about how more or different choices could be offered in the future.

VERBALISING YOUR DREAMS

Objective

For care workers to reveal their own ambitions.

Participants

Individual work; then sharing in pairs. Ideally, the pairs should be made up of people who do not know each other very well.

Equipment

Paper and pens.

Time

10 minutes for individual work; 15 minutes in pairs.

Task

Individual work

1. Take a few minutes to think about things that you would like to do in your life in the future in order to feel fulfilled by the time you retire.

2. Write a list of things which you would like to achieve (related to your personal life and work life).

3. Do you think you will be able to achieve your ambitions? If not, why is this?

Paired work

1. Tell your partner what your ambitions are and why you think you can or cannot achieve them.

2. Both of you should make suggestions about how these ambitions could be achieved.

Feedback

1. In the large group the pairs discuss how easy or difficult it was to talk about their dreams and ambitions to someone they did not know very well.

2. Discuss how a service user might feel talking about their private dreams to a care worker.

QUIZ SHEET 2.1

HAS A SERVICE USER THE RIGHT TO

1.	Go out of the home/day centre?	Yes/No/Don't know
2.	Shop?	Yes/No/Don't know
3.	Smoke?	Yes/No/Don't know
4.	Drink alcohol?	Yes/No/Don't know
5.	Have sex?	Yes/No/Don't know
6.	Vote?	Yes/No/Don't know
7.	Have money in a bank/building society?	Yes/No/Don't know
8.	Bet on horses?	Yes/No/Don't know
9.	Buy a lottery ticket?	Yes/No/Don't know
10.	Have a prostitute in the home?	Yes/No/Don't know
11.	Keep a pet in the home?	Yes/No/Don't know
12.	Do jury service?	Yes/No/Don't know
13.	Refuse to take medication?	Yes/No/Don't know
14.	Refuse to bath/wash?	Yes/No/Don't know
15.	Refuse to eat/drink?	Yes/No/Don't know
16.	Stay up all night?	Yes/No/Don't know
17.	Eat when and where they want?	Yes/No/Don't know
18.	Choose their own GP?	Yes/No/Don't know
19.	Cross-dress?	Yes/No/Don't know
20.	Self-harm?	Yes/No/Don't know

VALUES

- Privacy

- Dignity

- Independence

- Choice

- Rights

- Fulfilment

(From: Department of Health (1989)
Homes Are For Living In. London: HMSO.)

EQUAL OPPORTUNITIES

All service users should be treated equally regardless of:

- Age

- Gender

- Race

- Culture

- Religion

- Sexuality

- Disability

WHAT WOULD YOU DO IF?

1. You hear a service user say to another service user: 'I never call those black workers anything because I don't know who they are. They all look the same to me.'

2. Michael refuses to sit on the same table as Hans because 'he's a German'.

3. Edward tells you he will not be bathed by your male colleague because 'he is queer'.

4. You are on a break in the staff room. You hear two colleagues referring to a disabled service user as 'peg-leg'.

5. A temporary manager is giving you supervision. He starts making comments about service users (e.g. 'She's the one that hasn't got all the chairs round the table isn't she?') and staff ('She's a single parent – what can you expect?') which make you feel uncomfortable.

PROMOTE EQUAL OPPORTUNITIES BY

- Treating service users as individuals

- Not stereotyping or labelling service users

- Respecting the rights of service users

- Valuing the contribution service users can make to the home/day centre

- Empowering service users

WHEN A SERVICE USER NEEDS PRIVACY

Have you thought about:

- Bathing/toileting/dressing (Are there locks on doors?)

- Bedrooms (Do you always knock before entering? Do you go in at night when the service user is asleep?)

- Eating (Can meals be eaten away from the dining room?)

- Praying (Where can a service user pray?)

- Visitors (Are there private areas? Are 'Do not disturb' signs available?)

- GP/nurses (Is there a medical room they can use?)

- Receiving post (Where is the service user given their post?)

- Money (Where is a service user given their allowance? Where can money be kept?)

- Possessions (Can they be locked away?)

- Using the telephone (Can a service user be overheard when using the telephone?)

- Records (Are they stored safely? Where could a service user read them privately?)

- Sexual relationships (Can they be maintained without staff/service users gossiping?)

- Location of key worker sessions

THE CONVENTION RIGHTS

Article 2: Right to life

Article 3: Prohibition of torture

Article 4: Prohibition of slavery
and forced labour

Article 5: Right to liberty and security

Article 6: Right to a fair trial

Article 7: No punishment without law

Article 8: Right to respect for private
and family life

Article 9: Freedom of thought,
conscience and religion

Article 10: Freedom of expression

Article 11: Freedom of assembly
and association

Article 12: Right to marry

Article 14: Prohibition of discrimination

Article 16: Restrictions on political
activity of aliens

Article 17: Prohibition of abuse of rights

Article 18: Limitation on use
of restrictions on rights

BOUNDARIES OF CONFIDENTIALITY

A care worker needs to explain to a service user that confidentiality will be maintained wherever possible, but:

- Any information given to a care worker belongs to the agency/organisation *not* to the individual worker

- A worker will share information with the line manager

- In some circumstances confidentiality may have to be broken

GOOD PRACTICE TIPS

In order to promote all the principles of care, a care worker should:

- Get to know the service user

- Build up trust

- Learn about the service user's past life

- Gain understanding about a service user's previous lifestyle

- Encourage a service user to express their opinion/beliefs

- Find out what and who is important to a service user

- Have a flexible and creative approach

Case Study 2.1

Last week Alice was admitted to care having suffered a stroke. She needs help with personal care tasks. She gets very embarrassed whenever somebody has to help her to the toilet or have a bath. She has told staff that no one has ever seen her completely naked before – not even her husband. So far, female care workers have supported Alice with toileting and bathing. This week, a lot of staff are off sick due to the flu virus and agency staff have been brought in, some of whom are men. Alice refuses to be bathed or toileted by the male care staff.

Discuss

1. How can you reduce Alice's embarrassment?

2. How should the home respond to Alice's request not to be toileted or bathed by male care workers?

Case Study 2.2

Harry was new to the day centre. He had been resistant to the idea of attending the centre because he had started wetting himself but had not told anyone about this. On the first day he had an accident when he was playing dominoes with several other people at a table. You are the care worker he tells.

Discuss

1. What would you say to Harry when he tells you he has wet himself?

2. How would you maintain his dignity bearing in mind he is sitting with other service users?

3. What would you do if Harry did not want to change his underwear/clothes?

Case Study 2.3

Matilda has dementia and is severely confused. She cannot remember anything which has happened to her within a few minutes. She is also doubly incontinent. Today, she is in the lounge with other service users. Another service user complains that Matilda smells and it is making her feel sick. When you go to Matilda you see faeces and urine on the chair and floor. She refuses to move from the chair.

Discuss

1. What would you do first?
2. What would you say to Matilda?
3. What would you need to consider and do in relation to the other service users?

Case Study 2.4

Dorothy is 93 years old. She told her keyworker 'I've had routine in my life' and she wanted to maintain this as much as possible. She had always done her housework in the morning (without her make-up on), had lunch at 12.00 and then washed, put on her make-up and changed into her 'decent clothes'. She listened to *Woman's Hour* at 2.00 in the afternoon and had been outraged when the BBC changed the time. About once a month she writes to the BBC to continue to lodge her complaint.

Discuss

1. Would it be possible for Dorothy to maintain her routine in your home?

2. How would you support her?

Case Study 2.5

Mr and Mrs Saunders are an African Caribbean couple who came to live in England in the 1950s. They have always worked nights; Mr Saunders worked in the steel industry and his wife was a nurse. When they come into residential care they want to continue to live their lives as they always have done. This involves sleeping between 8.00a.m. and 4.00p.m. and staying up all night.

Discuss

1. If Mr and Mrs Saunders were admitted to your home would they be able to follow their previous routine?

2. What obstacles might there be?

3. What choices would you offer them?

Case Study 2.6

Wendy had not had a happy marriage and she openly admits that she was glad when her husband died. She talks about 'beginning to live my life when he'd gone. He controlled everything I did. I couldn't even pee without telling him.' Her husband had given her a specific amount of money on a Friday which had to last the week. After he died she had enjoyed being able to manage her own financial affairs and being able to choose what to spend her money on. She particularly liked being able 'to buy frivolous things I don't need'. Wendy is now going to be admitted to a home.

Discuss

1. What choices would you give Wendy about managing her financial affairs?

2. Make a list of questions you would like to ask her about money, shopping, services she needs and things she likes to do.

Case Study 2.7

Katrina had spent a large part of her life in a mental institution where she had been admitted after getting pregnant at the age of 17. It was thought she had learning disabilities. She was released into the community in the early 1990s and it became clear to her social worker that she did not have learning disabilities. She has now been admitted to a home because she has had a stroke which has affected her physical mobility. In the last decade Katrina learnt that she had rights and she was eager to ensure that she was not deprived of her rights in the future. When she comes into the home she demands to see her file and wants to read all the reports which have been written, especially the ones from medical personnel. She is also eager to try to pursue getting access to her records from the mental institution and wants to find out what happened to her baby.

Discuss

1. What records has Katrina the right to see?

2. Would any reports be kept from her?

3. How would you help her in getting access to records from the mental institution?

4. Do you think there is any way of finding her child?

Case Study 2.8

Timothy was born in the local area where the care home is located. He spent most of his working life abroad and never kept in touch with his family because of an argument many years ago. He thinks that two of his brothers are still alive and may be living locally. He wants to try to find them.

Discuss

1. How would you go about helping Timothy find his living relatives?

2. What might you have to think about in regard to confidentiality?

3. What other work might you undertake with Timothy whilst trying to find his relatives?

Case Study 2.9

It is Malik Ali Rashid's first time at the day centre. The application form has little personal information about him. You know he is a Muslim and in his 70s. He has been in hospital recently (but you do not know why) and has agreed to attend day centre to give his family a break.

Discuss

1. What sort of things will you ask Malik Ali Rashid when he arrives at the day centre?

2. List things you *do* know about a Muslim person.

3. List things you *do not* know about a Muslim person.

4. How would you discuss issues surrounding the principle of fulfilment?

Chapter 3

Role of the Care Worker

Information in this chapter is relevant to:

TRAINING ORGANISATION for the PERSONAL SOCIAL SERVICES

TOPSS Induction Standard 1 – Understand the principles of care

  1.2 Worker relationships

TOPSS Induction Standard 2 – Understand the organisation and the role of the worker

  2.1   Access to policies and procedures

  2.2   Application of policies and procedures

  2.3   Role of the care worker

TOPSS Foundation Standard 3 – Develop as a worker

  3.2.2 Know the importance of maintaining a good diet and taking appropriate rest and relaxation when not at work

  3.2.3 Recognise the symptoms of stress and know what action to take in the event of this

NATIONAL VOCATIONAL QUALIFICATIONS

  O1   Foster people's equality, diversity and rights

  O2   Promote people's equality, diversity and rights

  CU7   Develop one's own knowledge and practice

  SC14 Establish, sustain and disengage from relationships with clients

  W1   Support individual in developing and maintaining their identity and personal relationships

  W2   Contribute to the ongoing support of clients and others significant to them

What is a care worker?

Today's use of the job title 'care worker' is rather broad, because it includes jobs within all different specialisms and settings. In relation to older people you could have a care worker working in home care services, or residential or day care settings. This chapter will look at the role of the care worker who may be working in a home or in a day centre. The title explains itself in that a care worker is there to care for service users, but the chapter will aim to look at what care is. The job involves a wide range of responsibilities and tasks, for which a person needs thorough and comprehensive training.

The job

Being a care worker should not be seen as 'just a job'; a good care worker will have commitment to the job and the service users they work with. Every job should have a clear job description and personal specification, so that anyone applying for a vacancy should be clear about what is expected of them. If a care worker has been working in a home or day centre for many years, a good manager would alert them to any changes in the job description. Bad practice can occur when a worker has worked in an establishment for a long time and thinks that s/he knows it all and avoids going on training courses.

People may have a stereotypical image of what a care worker might do in a caring role – 'they look after people'. This is true, but one needs to be clear about what 'care' means. It is not about 'becoming a friend'; a care worker needs to function within professional boundaries. The word 'care' can have different meanings.

Dictionary Definition

Care

The provision of what is necessary for the welfare of and protection of someone or something; serious attention or consideration applied to avoid damage, risk or error; feel concern or interest; look after and provide for the needs of.

It is not just about helping people with things they cannot do for themselves; the role of the care worker now goes much further than that. The main objective is to provide practical and emotional support through adopting the principles of care. The tasks go way beyond just providing for physical needs. The care worker has to work holistically to provide for needs which have been identified; this will be discussed in depth in the following chapter. Exercise 3.1 will encourage care workers to think about the qualities and skills that are needed to do the job.

Responsibilities

Dictionary Definition

Responsibility
The state or fact of being responsible; the opportunity or ability to act independently and take decisions without authorisation; a thing which one is required to do as part of a job, role, or legal obligation.

Task
A piece of work to be done.

It must be stressed that a care worker is accountable to a line manager, and if at anytime a worker is unsure about their role or whether they should do something in particular, then they should *always* ask for guidance.

Care workers have a number of important responsibilities. They are there to care for service users by:

- assessing risk and meeting needs
- acting in their best interests
- promoting their well-being
- empowering
- promoting health and safety.

Handout 3.1, p.95

There are a great number of tasks involved in caring for a service user. Exercise 3.2 aims to get care workers thinking about and clarifying their responsibilities and tasks. Sometimes a worker might take on something which they should not do as it is the responsibility of someone else; that is, they can go beyond their remit. A care worker should never work in isolation; they should liaise with colleagues within the work setting but also share what they are doing with their line manager in supervision (see Chapter 9). Handout 3.2 can be used in conjunction with local job descriptions; the list is not meant to be exhaustive.

The number of tasks which a care worker will have to perform is enormous and a new worker will learn a lot through doing the 'hands on' work. However, there are many rules and regulations which must be adhered to and a worker must have training on subject areas related to health and safety as soon as possible. Most of the subject areas are mentioned in the TOPSS Induction Standard 4 and cannot be covered in this training manual. Therefore, the reader should use the videos which have been produced to help meet the requirements of this Standard (see Video section at the end of this chapter and Appendix 1).

Starting the job

When a person is starting a job in a new setting they should have a proper induction, even if they have done this sort of work before. The induction should introduce the person to the job and workplace by giving information about:

- the organisation (employer)
- the place of work (home or day centre)
- responsibilities and tasks
- policies and procedures
- training.

Handout 3.3, p.97

Under the TOPSS requirements care workers will be expected to meet certain standards:

> Managers must ensure that all new staff complete the induction standards within the first six weeks of employment and the foundation standards within the first six months. They will need to be sure that there is a record of this available for use during inspections and that the staff themselves have their own record. (TOPSS 2001, p.6)

It should be made clear to the worker what is expected of them and what can be offered to them to support them and promote their professional development; that is, through supervision and training.

If a new care worker is not given the following items they should ask to see them:

- induction pack

- mission statement/brochure for home/day centre

- manual which includes all policies and procedures (or files in which larger documents are kept separately)

- annual training programme.

Handout 3.3, p.97

Someone who has never worked in the field of social care might feel quite over-whelmed in the first few days because there is so much to learn. They might feel quite pressurised because so much has to be learnt in the first six weeks. A manager and staff team should do everything they can to help and support the new worker. It is important to give information but not to bombard the worker with too much. Managers should give a great deal of thought to how information can be imparted creatively; that is, not just by telling and giving out lots of pieces of paper. The following can be used together:

- talking/discussions with colleagues and others

- books/articles

- shadowing colleagues

- attending different types of meetings (e.g. reviews, case conferences)

- training materials

- videos.

We all get nervous when we start something new. A care worker should be encouraged to vent any fears or anxieties they may have. Often it is the little things that are worrying but it seems stupid to ask about them (e.g. 'Where is the toilet?'). Exercise 3.3 should encourage workers to talk about their major and minor anxieties.

Working in partnership

The term 'working in partnership' is one of those terms that has been heard more in recent years. A care worker will work in partnership with many people, the primary

75

person being the service user. Historically, people have used (and still use) the term 'multi-disciplinary working'. Partnership promotes the idea of working together with someone on an equal basis; as has already been mentioned a care worker should remember that providing care is about working *with* service users – it is not something which is done *to* them. In order to provide good quality care the care worker will continually assess the needs of a service user; this will be done by monitoring and reviewing what is happening in a service user's life. A key objective must be to build trust and a good working relationship, otherwise a service user will not confide or talk to a care worker in an open and confident way. The main aim is to work towards a service user maintaining as much independence as possible, even when they are physically or mentally dependent.

The service user is of prime importance, but to work effectively a care worker is going to have to work in partnership with other people too:

- manager

- other staff in the home/day centre

- professionals

- workers from other organisations

- family of service user

- friends of service user

- volunteers

- advocates

- religious leaders

- entertainers/activities people

- other agencies/organisations

- people in the local community.

Handout 3.4, p.98

A care worker will be part of a team within the home or day centre. All of the team will have contact with service users no matter what capacity they work in. The team might include: the manager, senior staff, other care workers, minibus driver, escort, domestics, activities organisers, handyman/caretaker, gardener. There may be occasions when a care worker will have to liaise with other people within the organisation and this will differ depending on who the employer is (local authority, private company or voluntary organisation). Examples could be: owner, personnel department, other workers working in a different capacity within the organisation.

As we shall see in the following chapter an older person may have all sorts of needs. The home or day centre may be able to meet some needs but the care plan may require other professionals or organisations to be involved to meet specialised needs. Exercise 3.4 is designed to make care workers think of professionals in the broadest sense and to encourage them to voice how they view such people (that is, do they stereotype by profession?).

I often hear the comment: 'I'm only a care assistant.' I get very concerned when care staff regularly undervalue themselves. This attitude can emanate from being underpaid and not being given enough recognition for the valuable work they do. Care workers are the people who have in-depth knowledge about service users because they spend so much time with them. Yet they often feel intimidated by a person who is regarded as a professional. People tell me they feel inferior because: 'They speak posh, I don't'; 'He uses long words I don't understand'; 'She went to university, she must be clever.' Feeling like this can hinder working in partnership because a care worker may not feel confident in expressing their opinion. It is a very crucial part of the role of being a care worker to assess and share information. So who is a professional exactly?

Dictionary Definition

Professional
Relating to or belonging to a profession; engaged in an activity as a paid occupation rather than as an amateur; worthy of or appropriate to a professional person; competent.

The dictionary definition of 'professional' given above suggests that a care worker could be deemed as doing a professional job; we certainly encourage care staff to work within professional boundaries, as we shall see below. Exercise 3.4 is interesting to undertake because it teases out how workers really feel about certain professionals. Handout 3.5 lists the professionals a care worker could come into contact with; it can be used in conjunction with Exercise 3.4 or it can be used alone as a starting point for discussion. There are some people on the list whom a care worker might not immediately think about. The following case examples illustrate how these professionals might become involved.

Case Examples

- Mrs Ellis had been physically abused by her son and was admitted to a care home as a place of safety. The son found out where Mrs Ellis was and tried to enter the home; he became very violent and the police had to be called. He was known to the probation service; his probation officer contributed to the risk assessment and the case conference which was convened under the Vulnerable Adults Policy and Procedure.

- Jack's grandson was serving time in prison. Jack received a letter from his grandson saying he was on the hospital wing, but did not say why. He asked a day care worker to ring the prison to find out what was going on, which she did. By speaking to a prison officer she was able to arrange for Jack to have a pre-arranged telephone conversation with his grandson.

- Rachel had never made a will and wanted to do so. The care worker contacted a solicitor who came to visit Rachel in the home.

If a care worker is doing their job properly then it is likely that s/he will have to liaise with a wide range of people other than professionals. This happens in order to meet the wide range of needs of a service user which will be discussed further in the next chapter. For example, part of a care worker's role is to arrange activities for a service user both within and outside the home; a day care worker might become involved with people who are supporting a service user in the community.

Case Examples

- A fitness trainer came into a nursing home once a week to lead chairobics.

- Staff organised an evening of entertainment. They brought in a comedian and a piano player.

- Violet wanted to take holy communion once a month. The priest came in and also heard her confession.

- Beth was going to be keyworker for Percy who was African-Caribbean. She contacted the local West Indian Association for information.

- Mrs Hayward has communication difficulties, but she can talk a little bit. Her family were always complaining about the care staff and thought she was allowed 'too much freedom'. There was always conflict between the family, staff at the home and other professionals. It was decided Mrs Hayward should have an advocate to act on her behalf.

- Day centre staff talked to the continence nurse about how they could do some pelvic floor exercises with service users.

- Every month the day centre had a themed lunch. A group of English service users said they wanted to try 'proper Chinese food not take-away rubbish'. The cook contacted the local Chinese Association for information about authentic Chinese dishes.

- An aromatherapist came in to give a talk to day centre users about the use of essential oils.

None of us can know everything and it is important that a care worker takes time to obtain information to fill gaps in knowledge and understanding. Not everything can be learnt from supervision and training courses. The care worker needs to be pro-active in seeking out information. This can be obtained from a variety of sources:

- people – the service user, manager, colleagues, professionals, workers, training officers, NVQ assessors, advocates, volunteers, family, friends

- local communities/associations

- books/journals/magazines

- policies and procedures

- training manuals/materials

- specialist organisations – who may produce information sheets

- libraries

- Citizens' Advice Bureaux

- the Internet.

Handout 3.6, p.100

It must be realised that this aspect of the work takes time. Sometimes it is like being a detective; over time a care worker will develop skills to know where and how to find out things.

Not everyone is a great reader, so books and articles should never be loaded onto anyone. People cannot be forced to wade through written materials. However, short articles or snippets of information can be useful and should be placed or displayed somewhere for staff to see (for example, on a noticeboard in the staff room). It can be useful to develop a resource file so that care workers have somewhere central to go to for information. It is simple to create a resource file; an A4 lever arch file can be used to keep lists of useful people, contacts, organisations, leaflets etc. The resource file can be developed and expanded over time by subject area. It should be located in a central location where care workers can easily access it and not forget that it exists or for what purposes it can be used.

It concerns me when people refer to the Internet and make assumptions. I often hear trainers say 'You can download this from…' It should not be assumed that everyone is fortunate enough to have access to a computer or knows how to use the Internet. When I was researching for this manual, I contacted organisations to ask them to send me their information leaflets and publications list so I could read what was available before making recommendations in this manual. I was surprised how many organisations responded not by sending any information but suggesting I just refer to their website.

On a more positive note there are a lot of organisations who supply excellent information leaflets which will be of use to both service users and care staff. I have listed these in Appendix 2. Over the past twenty years I have always used the annual *Charities Digest*, which is a mine of information. A care worker can find out about a lot of organisations and what they do; for example, provide grants, organise holidays, provide information sheets. It is important to use both local and national resources/organisations. Many people within the community may have knowledge and expertise.

Exercise 3.5 is designed to develop a care worker's knowledge about where to obtain information. If care workers from different workplaces undertake this exercise together, they should be able to pool their ideas and develop their knowledge base.

Working with family and carers

So far working in partnership has been defined in terms of working with the service user, professionals, workers and organisations. Another aspect of the work is liaising with family, friends or other people who might have an important role to play in a service user's life. If a service user is mentally sound, then it is necessary to ask their permission to talk to the people concerned. Not all families get on, so a service user might not want information shared with certain people. If a service user is mentally incapacitated, after discussion with a manager it may be deemed helpful to talk to people who knew the service user before they became incapacitated. These people may have information about previous lifestyle, key events in the service user's life etc.

A care worker can encourage family and carers to become involved in the life of the service user and the home/day centre by participating in:

- visits
- reviews
- relatives' support groups
- activities.

The Relatives and Residents Association have an extensive list of publications which could be of use both to care workers and relatives. One in particular is *Involving Relatives and Friends: A Good Practice Guide for Homes for Older People* (Burton-Jones 2001).

Keyworker

Many homes and day centres operate a keyworker system. This is where a service user is allocated a care worker who is the 'special worker'; that is, they are responsible for working closely with the service user. Every member of staff should know all the service users they work with, but the keyworker will have special responsibility for developing a care plan for a service user, which is then used by all staff. The main objective is to try to build a close relationship on a one to one basis. Most people do not want to repeat things several times over; neither do they feel comfortable nor trust everyone equally. A keyworker is usually appointed as soon as a service user is admitted to a home or starts attending a day centre. Sometimes a service user will request a change of keyworker if s/he feels she cannot get on with them. These wishes should be respected, thus promoting the principle of choice.

A care worker should understand fully their role as keyworker. It is useful to read the research study by Mallinson (1995), *Keyworking in Social Care: A Structured Approach to Provision*, and Coleman, Regan and Smith (1999), *Who Care Plans*. The latter made a recommendation regarding keyworker systems which includes explicit detail of tasks which should be undertaken:

9. The keyworker system

It is helpful for each resident to have a keyworker, named nurse or equivalent, who should be an experienced member of staff who takes a special responsibility for that resident's care.

- The tasks of keyworkers in relation to care planning should be carefully identified and documented by managers.

- In homes where there are named nurses as well as keyworkers, care should be taken to ensure that their respective duties are particularly carefully defined so as to enhance the professional responsibility of the qualified nurse without undermining the status and motivation of the keyworker.

- Keyworkers should as far as possible be matched with residents, and residents should have the right to veto a keyworker with whom they do not feel comfortable.

- Keyworkers should be closely involved in any significant development in the care of the residents for whom they take special responsibility.

- Provision should be made for keyworkers' observations and comments to be captured in clients' records even if the keyworker is not authorised to enter material personally.

- The keyworker system and the respective staff responsibilities should be clearly explained to residents, relatives and others involved in residents' care.

(Coleman *et al.* 1999, p.73)

At the outset a care worker should explain clearly to the service user the role of a keyworker and the boundaries of that relationship. The service user needs to understand that the time put aside for a keyworker session is allocated to talk about how things are going generally; problems which have arisen can be highlighted; work can be undertaken on special agreed areas (e.g. making a lifestory book). It should also be made clear that although the sessions are specially designated, a service user can talk to the keyworker about issues at anytime or to another member of staff. The boundaries of confidentiality should be clearly explained and repeated at regular intervals.

A keyworker session should be conducted privately and should never be rushed or 'fitted in'. I have seen a lot of bad practice where a keyworker session has taken place in a public place; for example, the keyworker and service user sitting in a circle with other day centre users. The sessions should be booked in advance and duration and time decided in conjunction with the service user.

Professional boundaries

I train a lot of care workers who have worked with their service users for years and in some cases it becomes very evident that the workers have got their boundaries muddled: 'They're just like family to me.' It cannot be emphasised enough that service users are *not* family. Care workers have to be very clear that they are doing a job when caring for service users. Care workers cannot be replacements for what is missing in a service user's life; for example, family or friends. Alternatively, service users should not be a replacement for what is missing in a care worker's life. A care worker sometimes goes beyond the job's remit or call of duty. They may 'do little things' in their own time for the service user.

Emotions will come into play whilst doing the job; strategies have to be developed to cope with these. It is important not to get too emotionally involved and to be able to cut off. A care worker should be encouraged to vent feelings, but again this needs to be done in a professional way. Whatever emotion affects a care worker it should be talked about with a manager or colleague before going off shift. Excess baggage should never be taken home. Sometimes things do stay with you, but no care

Case Example

Betty was 45 years old and recently divorced; all her children had left home. She became a care worker in order 'to have a fresh start and do something with my life'. She loved the job and did well, but it came to take over her life. She always volunteered to work extra shifts, cover for sickness/holidays and then she got in the habit of dropping in to the home on her days off 'because I have nothing else to do'.

worker should be having sleepless nights worrying about a work issue; neither should they discuss work matters at home because of breaking confidentiality. It also works the other way: a care worker should not say too much about their personal/family life to service users. Handout 3.7 and Quiz Sheet 3.1 may raise some interesting discussion about boundaries.

Caring for self

Care workers care for service users, but they must also care for themselves. Being a care worker can be a demanding job both physically and emotionally. If you are working excessively hard over a period of time, then there will be an effect on both your body and mind. I think the word 'stress' is overused nowadays, but its true meaning is a valuable focal point when assessing what is happening in your life.

Dictionary Definition

Stress

A state of mental, emotional or other strain.

People experience the effects of 'being stressed' in different ways: being bad-tempered; no patience; not sleeping; lack of concentration; no energy; depression. The saying 'Prevention is better than cure' should be contemplated. None of us are superhuman. Even if someone is a very strong person who puts everybody else before themselves and whom everyone relies on, there is going to be a breaking point. The importance of self care cannot be emphasised enough – we all need to regularly eat properly, exercise, relax and sleep.

Home and work must be separated. In order to cut off from work it is helpful to have interests and relationships which will distract from work. People have different ways of taking their mind off things and/or relaxing. A young care worker who goes home to a husband and three children under the age of five is immediately going to have her mind occupied by something completely different after a shift. For Betty, in the case example above, it was a different story: she had no friends or interests outside work. It is good to have family and friends who are not connected to work. People who only socialise with people working in the same field end up talking about work matters, which is not healthy. A real warning sign that a care worker is not looking after themselves is when they say: 'I feel too tired to do anything for myself.' Undertaking Exercise 3.6 is a good way of making a care worker face the possibility that s/he is not looking after themselves very well.

Suggested reading

Burton-Jones, J. (2001) *Involving Relatives and Friends: A Good Practice Guide for Homes for Older People.* London: The Relatives and Residents Association.

Charities Digest

Coleman, V., Regan, D. and Smith, J. (1999) *Who Care Plans.* London: Counsel and Care.

Howard, H. (2000) *The Care Assistant's Handbook.* London: Age Concern England.

Mallinson, I. (1995) *Keyworking in Social Care: A Structured Approach to Provision.* London: Whiting and Birch.

Useful organisations

The following two organisations provide excellent information about all aspects of care and have publication lists. Care workers will not only gain useful knowledge, but will develop new ideas about ways of working.

National Association for Providers of Activities for Older People (NAPA)

5 Tavistock Place, London WC1H 9SN
Tel/Fax: 020 7383 5757

The Relatives and Residents Association

5 Tavistock Place, London WC1H 9SN

Tel: 020 7692 4302 Fax: 020 7916 6093 Advice Line: 020 7916 6055

E-mail: relres@totalise.co.uk

VIDEOS

Role of the Care Worker

The following videos will help care workers in regard to their responsibilities regarding health and safety issues, which are part of TOPSS Induction Standard 4 – Maintain Safety at Work:

Emergency First Aid

Fire Drills and Evacuation

Fire Prevention

Food Hygiene

Health and Safety

Moving and Handling

WHAT MAKES A GOOD CARE WORKER?

Objective

To focus care workers on the qualities and skills needed to be a good care worker.

Participants

Small groups.

Equipment

Flipchart paper and pens.
Photocopies of local job descriptions.

Time

20 minutes.

Task

1. Imagine that you have been asked to write a job description which could be used to advertise the job of care worker in your place of work.

2. Discuss what makes a good care worker.

3. Make a list of personal *qualities* you think a care worker should possess.

4. Make a list of *skills* a care worker should have.

Feedback

1. Each group presents their list.

2. Trainer gives out local/organisational job description(s), which are then compared to the lists and discussed in full.

RESPONSIBILITIES AND TASKS

Objective

To clarify the roles and responsibilities of a care worker.

Participants

Small groups.

Equipment

Flipchart paper and pens.
Photocopies of local job descriptions.
Copies of Handout 3.2.

Time

20 minutes.

Task

1. Discuss and list the main *responsibilities* a care worker has in your work setting.

2. Discuss and list the main *tasks* you perform in your job every shift.

Feedback

1. Each group presents their lists.

2. Trainer gives out local/organisational job description(s) and Handout 3.2, which are then discussed.

THINGS I'M WORRIED ABOUT

Objective

To give a new care worker the opportunity to be honest about the things which are worrying them.

Participants

Individual and group work.

Equipment

Post-It stickers (76mm x 76mm).
Cardboard box.
Clear wall.

Time

5 minutes.

Task

1. Participants are given 5 Post-It stickers each.

2. They are asked to write down their anxieties or something they do not know, which is bothering them. Each anxiety or question should be written on a separate sticker. (Participants do not have to use all the stickers or they can ask for more stickers if they need them.)

3. The trainer collects the stickers in the cardboard box and then puts them up on a wall. Participants walk round the room to read the stickers on the wall.

Feedback

1. Discussion follows about the types of anxieties and questions that have been raised.

2. Trainer asks whether anyone in the group can comment on or answer the queries.

3. Trainer responds when participants cannot.

Note for trainer

It should be emphasised that participants are being asked to be honest and the use of Post-It stickers and the cardboard box is to maintain anonymity.

WHO IS A PROFESSIONAL?

Objective

To get care workers to think about who they would classify as being a 'professional' person and to bring out any stereotypical images of such people.

Participants

Small groups.

Equipment

Flipchart paper and pens.
Copies of Handout 3.5 if required.

Time

15 minutes.

Task

1. Think about professional people you might have to liaise with in your job.

2. List the people you thought of.

3. Discuss any views or opinions you have of them.

Feedback

1. Groups go through their lists.

2. Lists are compared.

3. Stereotypes are discussed.

4. Handout 3.5 can be used to further discussion.

THINK OF A GAP

Objective

To get care workers to think creatively about getting information.

Participants

Individual and group work (4 per group).

Equipment

Paper and pens.
Flipchart paper and pens.

Time

5 minutes for individual work; 40 minutes for group work (10 minutes on each 'gap' identified).

Task

1. Each care worker has to identify a gap in their knowledge. This could be something from the past which has occurred when working with a service user or a subject area which they know nothing about now. The worker writes the gap down on a piece of paper.

2. The trainer then puts the workers into groups of 4 with sheets of flipchart paper (one for each gap).

3. Each group is asked to work on the 4 gaps they have identified. They list people, places and organisations they would go to get information.

Feedback

1. Groups present their gaps and ideas.

2. The trainer writes a list of resources/organisations as the groups are feeding back. This list is typed up and sent out to participants after the course has finished. Such lists can be put in a resource file.

SELF CARE

Objective

To get care workers to think about how they cut off from work and how they currently look after themselves. To develop a self care action plan.

Participants

Individual work and then sharing in pairs.

Equipment

Self Care Questionnaire (Handout 3.8) to be photocopied by trainer.

Time

10 minutes to complete questionnaire.

Task

1.   Complete questionnaire.

2.   Share with one other person (e.g. another participant on course or line manager in supervision).

Feedback

Group discussion on how to self care.

QUIZ SHEET 3.1

PROFESSIONAL BOUNDARIES

Would you:

1. Talk about your family to a service user?   Yes/No/Maybe

2. Discuss a service user/what happened at
   work with a family member/friend?   Yes/No/Maybe

3. Tell a service user when your birthday is?   Yes/No/Maybe

4. Send a service user a birthday card from
   you personally?   Yes/No/Maybe

5. Bring a service user a present from
   your holidays?   Yes/No/Maybe

6. Accept a present from a service user
   or their family?   Yes/No/Maybe

7. Discuss with a service user a problem
   you have at home?   Yes/No/Maybe

8. Talk about a personal matter which
   has happened to you in the past?   Yes/No/Maybe

9. Talk about any medical problems you
   have or have had?   Yes/No/Maybe

10. Take a service user to visit your home?   Yes/No/Maybe

11. Bring a family member in to meet service
    users?   Yes/No/Maybe

12. Let a service user give your child a
    £1 coin?   Yes/No/Maybe

13. Recommend a relative/friend to provide
    a service (e.g. gardening, decorating) for
    a service user or someone they know?   Yes/No/Maybe

14. Use your own reward card when you
    shop for service users?   Yes/No/Maybe

15. Borrow money from a service user?   Yes/No/Maybe

16. Let a service user put you in their will?   Yes/No/Maybe

17. Let a service user buy you a drink in the
    local pub?   Yes/No/Maybe

18. Cry in front of a service user?   Yes/No/Maybe

19. Talk about another service user in front
    of a service user?   Yes/No/Maybe

20. Let a service user tell you a dirty joke?   Yes/No/Maybe

RESPONSIBILITIES

A care worker is there to care for service users by:

- Assessing risk and meeting needs

- Acting in their best interests

- Promoting their well-being

- Empowering

- Promoting health and safety

CHECKLIST: POSSIBLE TASKS

- Washing/bathing/toileting
- Dressing/undressing
- Feeding
- Administering medication
- Moving a service user
- Walking with a service user
- Talking/listening
- Reading/writing
- Finding out about a service user
- Developing trust
- Developing a working relationship with a service user
- Being a keyworker/organising keyworker sessions
- Observing service users
- Providing stimulation
- Organising activities/events
- Liaising with other people
- Communicating – verbally/non-verbally/in writing
- Keeping records
- Providing/working within a safe environment
- Responding to accidents/giving first aid
- Participating in meetings
- Providing information
- Participating in supervision
- Attending training courses

WHEN YOU ARE NEW

When a care worker starts a new job they need to be given information about the following:

- The organisation (employer)

- The place of work (home or day centre)

- Responsibilities and tasks

- Policies and procedures

- Training

Care worker should be given to read:

- Induction pack

- Mission statement/brochure for home/day centre

- Manual which includes all policies and procedures (or files in which larger documents are kept separately)

- Annual training programme

WORKING IN PARTNERSHIP

- Manager

- Other staff in the home/day centre

- Professionals

- Workers from other organisations

- Family of service user

- Friends of service user

- Volunteers

- Advocates

- Religious leaders

- Entertainers/activities people

- Other agencies/organisations

- People in the local community

TRADITIONAL PROFESSIONALS

- GP

- Doctors in hospital

- Nurses – hospital and community

- Pharmacist

- Psychologists

- Psychiatrist

- Physiotherapist

- Speech therapist

- Occupational therapist

- Dietician

- Chiropodist

- Dentist

- Optician

- Religious leader

- Probation officer

- Prison officer

- Police

- Solicitor/Barrister

GETTING INFORMATION AND GAINING KNOWLEDGE

- People – the service user, manager, colleagues, professionals, workers, training officers, NVQ assessors, advocates, volunteers, family, friends

- Local communities/associations

- Books/journals/magazines

- Policies and procedures

- Training manuals/materials

- Specialist organisations – who may produce information sheets

- Libraries

- Citizens' Advice Bureaux

- The Internet

PROFESSIONAL BOUNDARIES

In order to remain within professional boundaries it is good practice for a care worker:

- To talk about how they feel to a manager or colleague before they go home

- Not to discuss work matters at home

- To develop ways of cutting off from work

SELF CARE QUESTIONNAIRE

1. Do you find it difficult to cut off from work? (If you do, what do you find yourself thinking about most?)

2. What helps you to cut off from work (e.g. people, activities)?

3. Do you think work affects your personal life? (If so, in what way(s)?)

4. Would you say you are a person who 'gets stressed'? (If so, how does stress affect you?)

5. Do you have interests and hobbies that you do not do enough? (If yes, what are they?)

6. What do you like doing to relax?

7. Do you ever treat or pamper yourself? (If yes, how and how often? If no, why not?)

8. If you do not want to think about something or someone, what do you do?

9. Do you think you need to take better care of yourself?

10. List 5 things you need to do in the next month which will promote taking better care of your physical and mental well-being.

(a)

(b)

(c)

(d)

(e)

Chapter 4

Needs of Older People

The TOPSS Induction Standard 3.1 requires a care worker to understand the types of service user groups. This manual is concerned with older people – therefore, this chapter will only be concerned with this particular service user group. However, mention will be made of particular problems which might relate to other service user groups; that is, learning disabilities and mental health problems. Older people could experience these difficulties in later life and had they been under 65 would have come under a different service user group.

It is important to state at the beginning of this chapter that certain conditions and disabilities will be mentioned and references and sources will be given so that care workers can increase their knowledge in the future. It would be an impossible task to write about everything in depth within the chapter. My main aim is to alert care workers to the fact that they should be looking at 'needs' in the broadest sense. Certain subject areas which could be identified as needs are considered in depth in later chapters; for example: challenging behaviour, death, dying and bereavement.

The image of older people

The image of an older person is often negative in this society. Old age is associated with decline in physical and mental health, illness, inability to do things – the list goes on. We can all think of terms that are used about older people which contribute to a negative image – 'geriatrics', 'frail elderly', 'elderly mentally infirm'. When advertisements appear in magazines and newspapers with older people in them, they are usually advertising stairlifts, continence aids, hearing aids, remedies for hair loss. Rarely do we see photographs of fit and healthy older people.

Task

Pick up a magazine or newspaper and look at the advertisements. How many can you find which give a positive image of an older person? How many give a negative image?

A typically ageist view is that older people are a costly burden on society; they do not produce anything and increase national expenditure because of the costs of providing state pensions, their need for health care and other services. This is not true of every older person, it is a generalisation.

Consequently, many people fear growing old or do not want to work with older people because they remind them of what is to come. The reality is that many older people are perfectly fit and well, and lead very active and rewarding lives. It is important not to see all older people as being the same. It must be remembered that they are all individuals and will experience old age differently; consequently they will present with different needs. These needs should be met by offering appropriate services, some of which may be offered to younger adults. Recent research found that older victims of abuse were not offered the same services (e.g. counselling and therapy) as younger victims of child abuse/domestic violence (Pritchard 2000). Some services had been denied on grounds of age.

Older people can offer a lot to younger generations: they are sources of wisdom and knowledge; they can inform and entertain us about the past. Working with older people can be very satisfying as well as rewarding; such jobs should not be seen as inferior. Being old should not be seen as 'the end'; as we saw in Chapter 2 a care worker should be striving to help an older person achieve fulfilment – that is, work towards some objectives or ambitions.

The ageing population

Around the world people are living longer. The oldest people in the world are two women who live in Dominica in the West Indies. The eldest is Elizabeth Pampo Israel, who became 128 years old on 27 January 2003. In the United Kingdom, women are currently considered to be of pensionable age at 60 and men at 65. Within agencies, older people are usually defined as being over 65. They form nearly a fifth of our population. In the year 2000, the population of the United Kingdom was estimated to be 59,756,000, of which 10,789,000 (18.1%) were people of pensionable age: 6,914,000 were women aged over 60 (of whom 5,442,000 were over 65) and 3,875,000 were men aged over 65 (*Population Trends* 2001).

In 1996, 5523 people in England and Wales were aged over 100. It is estimated that by 2036 this will have increased to 39,000 and to 95,000 in 2066 (*Population Trends* 1999). Life expectancy has also increased in recent years; in 1998 men were expected to live to 79, women to 82.6 (*Population Trends* 1999).

The ageing population is due to improvements in diet, increased medical research and knowledge, improved health care and facilities and changes in lifestyles.

Through the media we are encouraged to eat well and take exercise. Older people may have experienced very different lifestyles in their younger days; some of them may have experienced both World Wars, where food and other goods were rationed.

Older people today are living through many changes, especially in their experience of later adulthood but also in the meaning of old age. Perception is important. A teenager sees their middle aged parents as 'old'. A 65-year-old person may regard him/herself as 'young' but an 85-year-old person as 'old'.

Sometimes it is more convenient to slot things into categories. Organisations may divide people into categories too. For example, an insurance company may see a young male car driver under 25 as a high risk; a 45-year-old female driver may be considered a low risk. Social services departments may divide people into service user groups – for example: children and families; adults with physical and sensory disabilities; adults with learning disabilities; adults with mental health problems; older people.

So how does an ageing population affect older people and society in general? We have seen above that society often has a stereotypical negative view of old age. Discrimination does exist; some older people are refused services on grounds of their age – for instance, medical treatment or attendance at a specialised day centre for people with mental health problems.

The Government has taken steps in recent years to combat this with the introduction of the *National Service Framework for Older People* (Department of Health 2001b); see the related website: www.doh.gov.uk/nsf/olderpeople.htm.

In the *National Service Framework for Older People* Standard One is 'Rooting Out Age Discrimination'.

The **aim** of the standard is:

To ensure that older people are never unfairly discriminated against in accessing NHS or social care services as a result of their age.

The **standard** is:

NHS services will be provided, regardless of age, on the basis of clinical need alone. Social care services will not use age in their eligibility criteria or policies, to restrict access to available services.

Rationale:

Fair access lies at the heart of good public services.
(Department of Health 2001b, p.16)

Older people themselves have to come to terms with the fact that they are living longer. If they have worked all of their life, it may be very hard to adjust to retirement. Also, if they have not been able to save for retirement, they may be finding it hard to manage financially and not be able to afford to do the things they would like to do. Later in life, an older person has to adjust to losing family and friends who die before them. So many adjustments have to be made in later adulthood – including perhaps accepting care from other people.

Defining needs

Dictionary Definition

Need

Circumstances in which a thing or course of action is required; a thing that is wanted or required; a state of poverty, distress, or misfortune.

The main role for a care worker is to help meet the needs of a service user. An assumption can be made that needs can be divided into physical and emotional, but this is too restrictive. It is often easier for a care worker to think about practical needs:

- accommodation
- warmth
- lighting
- clothing
- food/drink
- personal hygiene.

It is more difficult to define emotional needs; people often find these hard to verbalise or to explain exactly what they need. A care worker must also give thought to a service user's spiritual, religious and cultural needs. This is where a care worker may have gaps in knowledge and need to find out about service users who come from different backgrounds.

Then there are the taboo subjects – the ones that people do not like to talk about. Many people feel uncomfortable talking about the sexual needs of older people or sexuality issues. I come across care workers who get embarrassed talking on training courses about sexuality; how are they going to work with a service user who wants to talk about their sexual needs or difficulties? Again, it can be lack of knowledge which makes a care worker feel unsafe or threatened. It is good for care workers to rehearse situations which they may find themselves in. This can be done through examples which will be cited in Exercise 4.1 or in Role Play 4.1.

☺ **ROLE PLAY 4.1**

Care workers are to work in pairs or trios in order to do the role play. One worker will be a care worker, the other(s) will be the service user(s). The pair/trio are asked to role-play one of the following situations (that is, they need to focus on what would be said immediately after the situation arose):

- Female service user tells a care worker she gets sexually frustrated and needs to masturbate.
- Male service user says he wants to use a prostitute.
- Having knocked on the door, care worker walks into a bedroom to find two service users having sex. The male service user has dementia.
- Male service user is visited by his male partner; they kiss in the lounge and then sit holding hands.

Exercise 4.1 will draw out subject areas which make care workers feel uncomfortable or embarrassed. A care worker needs to acknowledge such areas and rehearse how they would deal with the situations which might make them feel such emotions.

It is important for a care worker to think about all the different needs a human being may have – remembering that each individual is unique. Care workers should think about their own needs and consider whether they are any different to those of a service user. Exercise 4.2 will help them to do this in a structured way, but should also bring out whether any stereotyping and labelling is evident.

It can be helpful to put some structure to defining need. The Care Management and Assessment process is one such starting point. Need was described in various ways in guidance produced by the Department of Health: 'dynamic', 'a relative concept', 'a multi-faceted concept' and 'a complex concept'. The general definition given was:

> The requirements of individuals to enable them to achieve, maintain or restore an acceptable level of social independence or quality of life, as defined by the particular agency or authority. (DH 1991, p.12)

Six broad categories were given:

- personal/social care

- health care

- accommodation

- finance

- education/employment/leisure

- transport/access.

Handout 4.1, p.127

Standard 3 of the National Minimum Standards is concerned with **needs assessment**:

NATIONAL MINIMUM STANDARDS

3.1 New service users are admitted only on the basis of a full assessment undertaken by people trained to do so, and to which the prospective service user, his/her representatives (if any) and relevant professionals have been party.

3.2 For individuals referred through Care Management arrangements, the registered person obtains a summary of the Care Management (health and social services) assessment and a copy of the Care Plan produced for care management purposes.

3.3 For individuals who are self-funding and without a Care Management Assessment/Care Plan, the registered person carries out a needs assessment covering:

- personal care and physical well-being

- diet and weight, including dietary preferences

- sight, hearing and communication

- oral health
- foot care
- mobility and dexterity
- history of falls
- continence
- medication usage
- mental state and cognition
- social interests, hobbies, religious and cultural needs
- personal safety and risk
- carer and family involvement and other social contacts/relationships.

(DH 2002, p.3)

To have a framework to work to is useful, but the reality is that everyone will have different perceptions of need and many needs might fit under different headings. There is also the danger that by following standard categories of need, a care worker can start working in a set way and not be creative in the way they think. As has already been stated workers may find addressing certain needs (e.g. sexual) difficult or avoid issues because of their own lack of knowledge and confidence (e.g. about cultural or religious needs). Exercise 4.3 will help care workers draw out their perceptions regarding the different types of needs their service users might have.

A care worker must be reminded that needs presented by a service user may have to be met by a range of providers; that is, not just staff within the home or day centre. Specialised help may be required (for example, from a counsellor, psychologist, medical person) or some activity/interest might not be available in the home (for example, religious service, aromatherapy massage). Exercise 4.4 will take care workers one step further on from identifying the different types of needs, because the main task is to consider how needs can be met.

The National Minimum Standards consider needs of service users under two sections: **Health and Personal Care (Standards 7–11)** and **Daily Life and Social Activities (Standards 12–15)**. As stated earlier it is impossible to consider every possible need in one chapter, so some common needs will be discussed below.

Personal care

In the previous chapter attention was given to the fact that a care worker might be involved in all sorts of tasks when at work. Many of these tasks will be related to supporting a service user with personal care. Some service users may be able to do some things for themselves but require help with others, whereas someone who is profoundly disabled may require a great deal of support with most tasks.

Once a care worker gets used to doing the job some aspects of it can become routine. Therefore, it is imperative that a care worker reminds him/herself that a new service user might find the experience of being helped quite traumatic. A whole gamut of emotions could be presented – a service user may:

- feel embarrassed about another person seeing their body
- be uncomfortable being helped by someone of the opposite sex
- express anger or resentment because they have to be helped
- feel helpless.

A care worker needs to think about a lot of things, including:

- the feelings/emotions of the service user
- promoting privacy and dignity
- encouraging the service user to do as much as s/he can for her/himself
- health and safety issues
- acknowledging differences.

Handout 4.3, p.129

Case Examples

- Mrs Udin did not want male workers to toilet or bath her; it was not acceptable in her culture.

- Harriet had had a mastectomy; she did not like anyone to see her naked.

- Bernard liked to empty his colostomy bag himself.

- Rita was angry that staff said she had to use the hoist to be lifted for health and safety reasons. Rita said it made her feel like 'an invalid'.

Many needs will be interlinked and all of them will be addressed in the care plan. A care worker will have to constantly think about moving and handling issues together with health and safety issues when assessing needs. It would be useful to show the videos related to these areas of practice so that they are included when considering the needs of service users (see Video section at the end of the chapter).

Emotional needs

It would be impossible for anybody to predict all the emotional needs which could be presented by a service user – we all experience so many emotions on a daily basis and through life generally. However, care workers should be mindful of common emotions which they might come across more regularly:

- loss (see Chapter 11) – loss of home, lifestyle, independence, control, confidence, death of friend/relative
- disorientation/confusion when finding their way around a new place
- fear – about what is going to happen in the future
- frustration – not being able to do things
- shame
- embarrassment
- anger – perhaps at family for placing them in a home; about having a disability
- need to talk about feelings regarding events, incidents, unresolved issues from past life experiences

- sadness, upset
- depression.

It should not be forgotten by a care worker that a service user will experience happy emotions too!

Cultural, religious, spiritual needs

Case Examples

- Mr Sandhu, who was a Sikh, started having respite care in a home. None of the staff knew anything about the five religious symbols which were important to him. Mr Sandhu became very distressed before going to bed when staff tried to remove his Karra (steel bangle) from his wrist and Kirpan (small dagger) from his waist. He was also offended when his own underwear (Kachha) was not returned to him.

- Julie had just started to work in the kitchen which cooked for the home and day centre attached to it. The cook told her that two service users would not need any halal meat for lunch because it was Ramadan. Julie had to admit she did not know what the cook was talking about.

- The manager of a home changed one of the small lounges into a prayer room, so that the Muslim service users could go in there when they needed to pray (five times a day).

- Sadie Bell was African Caribbean. She explained to her keyworker that she needed to plait her hair each night before going to bed and 'cream meself'. Sadie's daughter brought in special creams and hair products for her mother and she showed staff how to plait hair for times when her mother was too tired to do it.

These types of needs are never given enough attention. It is interesting that in years gone by they were not mentioned specifically in any guidance on assessment, but assumed to be covered under personal needs. One particular point which is made throughout this manual is that a care worker cannot know everything, but s/he needs to be pro-active in finding out things when situations arise. If a service user from another country or different ethnic background starts attending a day centre or comes to live in a home it is imperative that staff find out as much as possible about that person's needs. There could be differences or special requirements regarding:

- dress

- diet

- washing

- prayers

- customs.

A care worker should contact national or local organisations for information when required or read informative books (Alibhai-Brown 1998; Henley and Schott 1999).

Health care

Health needs could be physical or mental. A care worker will be dealing with very basic health needs like personal and oral hygiene, prevention of pressure sores, provision of a healthy diet and exercise, organising hearing/sight tests etc.; but more complex health needs might also have to be met. There are so many medical conditions that a service user may have – each one presenting different needs. If a service user does have a medical condition it is important that a care worker understands what may be required. This is when it is important to contact people with specialist knowledge or national organisations for simple information leaflets (see Appendix 2).

A care worker will have to deal with what might be deemed 'common problems' on a day to day basis; for example, continence problems, administering medication. Every care worker needs training on these issues so that they have a basic understanding. Regarding continence, a care worker should know that there are different types of continence and there may be various causal factors. It is important to find out whether the problem is physical or psychological in order to develop an appropriate way of managing the problem.

Training on how to administer medication is crucial. Some service users will be able to manage and take medication themselves. However, others will need help. Where a service user presents problems, for example refusing to take medication, a proper risk assessment must be undertaken which will include obtaining opinion and advice from a medical person, e.g. GP, consultant. It is important to find out whether a situation could become life-threatening if medication is not taken. For further discussion on risk assessment see Chapter 6.

Mental health

> People with a mental illness can experience problems in the way they think, feel or behave... Mental illnesses are some of the least understood conditions in society... For some people, drugs and other medical treatments are helpful, but for others they are not. Medical treatment may only be a part of what helps recovery, and not necessarily the main part. (MIND 2001, p.2)

Mental health is a huge topic on which care workers must have some basic training. The term 'mental health' still conjures up negative images and stereotypes regarding 'nutters', 'psychopaths', 'mad people', 'people who are off their trolley' etc. Mental health problems include a vast range of conditions ranging from all levels of depression through to schizophrenia, personality disorders and so on:

- anxiety
- panic attacks
- phobias
- depression
- manic depression
- schizophrenia.

Older people may have specialised needs if they have a history of mental health problems. Very often they may have been receiving specialised services (e.g. attendance at a mental health day centre; working with an outreach/support worker in the community), then as soon as they have turned 65 they have been transferred to the older people's services. It is to be hoped that with the introduction of the National Service Framework for Older People this will change; many older people who go into care or attend a day centre may present with mental health problems and need specialised support. It is useful for homes and day centres to have MIND's catalogue of publications and leaflets.

Disability

Disability is a very broad term; the three main types of disability a care worker is likely to work with are:

- physical
- sensory
- learning.

A number of older people will have had some form of disability through their life, but it may not necessarily have been diagnosed correctly and they may not have received help to deal with it. Others will become disabled in later life and will need support in coming to terms with this.

Physical disability

A person can have a physical disability from birth or as a result of a medical condition, effects of a stroke or an accident. A care worker will be concerned with how to work safely with a disabled person – that is, moving and handling issues will be important – as well as focusing on communication needs.

Sensory disability

Sensory disability refers to loss of one (or more) of the senses (sight, hearing, speech, touch, smell). When talking about sensory disability, most people tend to think about people who are deaf, blind or have no speech. It is incredibly hard for anyone who has all their five senses to imagine what it must be like to lose one of them. Understanding the needs of such service users is vital in order to provide a safe environment and quality of life. A care worker needs to spend time with the service user asking about their disability and how it affects their life. Staff need to look at their workplace and try to assess what may prove to be an obstacle or hindrance to the disabled person. This is considered in more detail in Chapter 7.

Learning disability

Learning disability is also a massive topic. Years ago people were sometimes referred to as being 'ESN', which stood for 'educationally sub-normal'. Some older people have learning disabilities but have never been properly assessed and have not received appropriate services. Learning disabilities are present from childhood, they are not something which can develop in adulthood. There are no official statistics about the number of people in the United Kingdom with learning disabilities – a general estimate is about 1.2 million (British Institute of Learning Disabilities 2001, p.1). The World Health Organisation defines learning disabilities as:

- a state of arrested or incomplete development of mind
- significant impairment of intellectual functioning
- significant impairment of adaptive/social functioning.

(BILD 2001, p.2)

Terms which a care worker might come across in regard to learning disability are:

- moderate
- severe
- profound.

These are linked to IQ tests. An older person who has a learning disability may have difficulty with communication, self care, health and safety.

Dementia

Dementia is a term which is used quite casually by many workers when someone is presenting as confused. This can be very dangerous, as confusion can be caused by all sorts of conditions – a simple chest infection, a urinary tract infection or a change in medication. It is very important to make sure a proper assessment is undertaken and a diagnosis given. Therefore, dementia is yet another area where care workers need specialised training. The Alzheimer's Society says:

> The term 'dementia' is used to describe the symptoms that occur when the brain is affected by specific diseases and conditions... Dementia is progressive – which means the symptoms will get worse. How fast dementia progresses depends on the individual. Each person is unique and will experience dementia in their own way. (Alzheimer's Society 2001, p.1)

There are a number of diseases that can cause dementia, including:

- Alzheimer's
- vascular
- dementia with Lewy Bodies
- fronto-temporal dementia
- Korsakoff's syndrome
- Creutzfeldt-Jakob
- motor neurone
- multiple sclerosis
- Parkinson's
- Huntington's chorea
- HIV.

Dementia can affect both young and old people. It is estimated that there are about 750,000 people in the UK with dementia (about 17,000 are under 65). More and more work is being undertaken into understanding dementia, which has become a very specialised area of work. A care worker is not expected to learn everything, but some basic knowledge and understanding is vital in order to work well with service users. There are many useful sources of information. The Alzheimer's Society produces excellent information sheets and advice sheets, which are extremely comprehensive and written in plain, straightforward language. It would be advisable for homes and day centres to obtain a set of these. Care staff might also find it useful to contact their nearest Dementia Care Centre. Mary Marshall set up the first such centre in Stirling which produces excellent information and publications (see Useful organisations section at end of chapter).

Other problems

At the beginning of the chapter it was made clear that it would be an impossible task to discuss every need a service user might present. However, it must be pointed out that some service users who come into a home or attend a day centre may hide certain facts or problems from care workers. Their behaviour may indicate that problems do exist. Care workers should be alert to the fact that some service users may have a problem related to:

- alcohol

- drug/substance misuse

- gambling

- abuse (past or present).

If a particular problem is identified and care staff feel out of their depth, help should be sought from a professional and/or an organisation that specialises in dealing with the problem (e.g. local alcohol advisory service or drug helpline). A care worker should contact their local voluntary action bureau who will have contact points for local voluntary organisations. These may even be compiled into a local directory.

Activities

As discussed at the beginning of this chapter it is very easy to focus on negative images of old age. Likewise, when thinking about the needs of older people a care worker may focus primarily on the 'problem areas', because many service users will be dependent. However, it is necessary to keep reminding care workers about the principle of fulfilment. As discussed in the previous chapter, a care worker should be finding out about a service user's past life, which will include information about their hobbies and interests. Wherever possible these interests should be maintained. It is very easy to stereotype older people as wanting to play bingo, watch old films or have a sing-song. Some older people will want to engage in these activities but a care worker should try to be more imaginative in what they offer service users and give them some choices. Exercise 4.5 may help staff to become more creative. Handout 4.4 shows the results of this exercise when it was undertaken with staff from a number of care homes and day centres in a large city.

Case studies

The case studies at the end of the chapter (pp.131–3) can be used to encourage care workers to identify needs but also highlight their gaps in knowledge.

Suggested reading

Alzheimer's Society (June 2001) Information Sheets. London: Alzheimer's Society.

British Institute of Learning Disabilities (July 2001) Fact Sheets. Kidderminster: BILD.

MIND (2001) *Understanding Mental Illness* booklet.

Sherman, B. (1999) *Sex, Intimacy and Aged Care.* London: Jessica Kingsley Publishers.

Useful organisations

See Appendix 2 for a comprehensive list of organisations concerned with specific conditions. The following organisations may be of particular use:

Alzheimer's Society

Gordon House, 10 Greencoat Place, London SW1P 1PH

Tel: 020 7306 0606 Fax: 020 7306 0808

E-mail: info@alzheimers.org.uk Website: www.alzheimers.org.uk

British Institute of Learning Disabilities (BILD)

Campion House, Green Street, Kidderminster, Worcestershire DY10 3PP

Tel: 01562 723025 Fax: 01562 723029

E-mail: enquiries@bild.org.uk Website: www.bild.org.uk

MIND (National Association for Mental Health)

15–19 Broadway, London E15 4BQ

Tel: 020 8519 2122 Fax: 020 8522 1725 Mindinfoline: 0845 766 0163

E-mail: enquiries@mind.org.uk Website: www.mind.org.uk

National Association for Providers of Activities for Older People (NAPA)

5 Tavistock Place, London WC1H 9SN

Tel/Fax: 020 7383 5757

RNIB (Royal National Institute of the Blind)

105 Judd Street, London WC1H 9NE

Tel: 020 7388 1266 Fax: 020 7388 2034 Helpline: 0845 766 9999

E-mail: helpline@rnib.org.uk Website: www.rnib.org.uk

RNID (Royal National Institute for Deaf and Hard of Hearing People)

19–23 Featherstone Street, London EC1Y 8SL

Tel: 0808 808 0123 Textphone: 0808 808 9000 Fax: 020 7296 8199

E-mail: informationline@rnid.org.uk Website: www.rnid.org.uk

Stirling Dementia Services Development Centre

University of Stirling, Stirling FK9 4LA

Tel: 01786 467740 Fax: 01786 466846

E-mail: mtm1@stirling.ac.uk

Website: www.stir.ac.uk/Departments/HumanSciences/AppSocSci/DS

Useful website

Department of Health, about the *National Service Framework for Older People*: www.doh.gov.uk/nsf/olderpeople.htm

VIDEOS

Needs of the Service User

Other videos which are related to the subject of needs and will further knowledge in this area:

Principles of Care

Health and Safety

Moving and Handling

Risk Assessment (Moving and Handling)

Risk Assessment (Health and Safety)

WHAT I CAN'T TALK ABOUT EASILY

Objective

To identify difficult subject areas.

Participants

Individual work, then work in pairs.

Equipment

Paper and pens.

Time

5 minutes for individual work to make a list; 10 minutes sharing in pairs; 10 minutes for each role play.

Task

1. Make a list of subject areas related to work, which you would find difficult to talk about with any of the following people: manager, colleague, professional, service user.

2. Share your list with one other person in the group with whom you feel comfortable.

3. Discuss why these subjects make you feel uncomfortable.

4. Each person picks one subject area from their list. With their partner they will then role-play that situation for 10 minutes.

5. Make a list of strategies developed from the two role plays.

Feedback

1. Participants are asked to feed back on how they dealt with the situations.

2. The trainer makes a list of strategies.

Notes for trainer

1. The trainer needs to explain how the role play will be undertaken, i.e. in a safe environment – no one will watch. Handout 1.1 (p.21) can be used.

2. Participants should understand that they can stop and start the role play and try out different ways of responding in the situation.

3. Strategies will include words, phrases, use of body language.

PERSONAL NEEDS

Objective

To consider whether a care worker's needs are any different to those of a service user.

Participants

Individual work, then small group work.

Equipment

Paper and pens.
Flipchart paper and pens.

Time

10 minutes for individual work; 30 minutes in groups.

Task

Individual work

1. Think back to yesterday and what you did during the day from the moment you got up to going to bed at night.

2. Make a list of your 'needs' from yesterday.

Small group work

1. Participants will share and discuss their lists.

2. On the flipchart paper divide the needs into groups and give them headings.

Feedback

1. Groups will go through their headings and lists of needs.

2. Open discussion about 'types of needs'.

3. Discussion about differences between participants' needs and those of service users.

IDENTIFYING NEED

Objective

To anticipate the types of need which might have to be met in a home or day centre.

Participants

Small groups.

Equipment

Flipchart paper and pens.

Time

30 minutes.

Task

1. Each small group will focus on one 'need'.

2. Participants will discuss what types of things they might have to deal with regarding this type of need.

3. How would the need be met?

4. Identify gaps in knowledge.

Feedback

1. Each group feeds back about the 'need' they worked on.

2. Other groups are asked for their ideas (i.e. has anything been missed?).

3. Open discussion about needs.

Note for trainer

The trainer can choose the types of need to be worked on; it is useful to include the basic needs and the ones which cause some difficulty. Handout 4.2 may offer some suggestions to the trainer.

MEETING NEEDS

Objective

To anticipate how needs can be met and by whom.

Participants

Small groups.

Equipment

Flipchart paper and pens.

Time

30 minutes.

Task

1. Think about your own service users.

2. Make a list of needs which your service users have (whether they are currently met or not).

3. Next to the need identified write the person or organisation who does meet the need or, if it has not been met, make suggestions of who could provide the appropriate resource.

Feedback

1. Each group presents their list of needs and of providers/resources.

2. The other groups add to each list compiled.

3. Trainer collects the lists of providers/resources which will be typed up and given to participants after the course.

WHAT DO YOU OFFER?

Objective

To get care workers to think about activities they offer service users in their workplace and to encourage them to be more imaginative in their approach.

Participants

Small groups.

Equipment

Flipchart paper and pens.
Copies of Handout 4.4 if required.

Time

20 minutes.

Task

1.   Write a list of activities you offer your service users in your home or day centre.

2.   Think about the service users you know really well. List any unusual interests or hobbies they have or have had in the past, which are not pursued at the moment.

3.   List any activities you would like to be able to offer in your home or day centre in the future.

Feedback

1.   Each group will feed back their list of activities.

2.   Trainer will get these lists typed up after the course and circulated to participants.

3.   Handout 4.4 can be given out after the exercise.

DEFINITION OF NEED

The following definition of need was given in guidance produced by the Department of Health in 1991 when the Care Management system was introduced.

The requirements of individuals to enable them to achieve, maintain or restore an acceptable level of social independence or quality of life, as defined by the particular agency or authority.

Six broad categories were given:

- Personal/social care

- Health care

- Accommodation

- Finance

- Education/employment/leisure

- Transport/access

(From: pages 12–13, Department of Health (1991) *Care Management and Assessment: Practitioners' Guide.* London: HMSO.)

TYPES OF NEEDS

- Personal

- Physical

- Emotional

- Sexual

- Health (this can be divided into physical and mental)

- Accommodation

- Transport

- Spiritual/religious

- Cultural

- Social

- Leisure/interests

- Employment

- Education

- Finance

- Carers

WHEN MEETING PERSONAL CARE NEEDS THINK ABOUT

- The feelings/emotions of the service user

- Promoting privacy and dignity

- Encouraging the service user to do as much as s/he can for her/himself

- Health and safety issues

- Acknowledging differences

ACTIVITIES OFFERED IN HOMES AND DAY CENTRES

- Arts and crafts
- Baking/cooking
- Beauty and grooming
- Bingo
- Cards
- Cinema/theatre
- Computer literacy
- Crosswords
- Dominoes
- Entertainment
- Games
- Gardening
- Group discussions
- Hair and nails
- Holidays
- Horoscopes
- Knitting
- Mosaics
- Narrow boat trips
- Newspapers
- Outings
- Parties
- Physical exercise
- Pottery
- Pub lunches/eating out
- Quizzes
- Reading/going to library
- Relaxation/yoga
- Reminiscence
- Shopping
- Sing-a-long
- Snooker
- Sweeps – sport
- Swimming
- Tea dances
- Themed events
- TV/video
- Washing

Case Studies

1. Jacob is 78 years old and has recently suffered a massive stroke, which has left him paralysed down his left side. He can speak but it is quite difficult to understand him, as his speech is very slurred. His wife visits him every day. Their only son lives 200 miles away.

2. Mrs Kingsley is a blind 70-year-old African Caribbean woman, who suffers with sickle cell anaemia. She has started to come in for regular respite care to give her family a break.

3. Roland has always lived by himself. Prior to coming in-to care he had lived in very squalid conditions (environmental health officers have visited on several occasions when neighbours have complained about smells from the house and being over-run with rats). Roland has had his left leg amputated. He refuses to wash, stays in the same clothes every day and will only eat with his fingers.

4. Cherry was involved in a car accident some years ago which left her physically disabled (she uses a wheelchair and needs help with personal care) and partially deaf. Her husband was killed in the crash. She becomes very depressed at certain times of the year and self harms by cutting herself.

5. Charles has had cancer of the bowel and liver during the past five years. He has got used to using his stoma care but is finding it hard to accept help from care staff now he has come to live in care. He is a practising Catholic and has always been interested in football and gardening.

6. Janina Sawiska is a Polish woman who can only speak a few words of English. Since her husband died she has become very isolated; she has no family or friends left. A social worker has persuaded her to attend a day centre after receiving a referral from the GP who is concerned about managing her diabetes.

7. Sarah openly talks to day centre workers about the physical abuse she experiences from her husband. She says he has been violent from the day they married. She refuses to do anything about the abuse because she believes it is her duty as a wife to stay with him. In recent months she has become more agitated and now when she comes to the day centre it is very obvious that she has been drinking.

8. Oscar has Down's syndrome and has started with dementia. He lives with his mother, who has recently had a mild stroke. Oscar has started attending the day centre two days a week.

9. Parveen Khan is a Muslim woman who is visiting the day centre to see whether she likes it. The referral form tells you that she is about 80 years old, has severe arthritis which affects her mobility, is doubly incontinent and has a rare blood disorder. She lives with her son and his family.

10. Bill has schizophrenia; he has attended a mental health day centre for the past ten years. He lives alone and has been well supported in the community by a series of outreach workers. As soon as he turned 65 he was transferred to the older people's services and had to change day centres. He no longer has contact with any of the workers he has known for years.

Discuss

1. What are your first thoughts having read the case study?

2. What might be the needs of this service user?

3. What would you want to ask the service user?

4. What else would you need to know?

5. Where would you go for more information?

6. How would you meet this service user's needs?

Chapter 5

Care Planning

Objective of care planning

Care planning is about devising a way in which to meet the health and social care needs of a service user; this will be done by formulating an individual care plan which sets out how this is to be achieved. Developing a care plan is a crucial part of working with a service user. It would be bad practice just to respond to a service user's needs as they occurred; planning is a way of undertaking preventative work. As we saw in the previous chapter a service user may have a wide range of needs, which must be met by the home or day centre. A care plan is a way of working out how to meet these needs, then monitoring and reviewing what is happening to the service user over a period of time. Kina Avebury made a thoughtful comment which care workers should reflect on:

> Care planning sounds so easy, and so many people in the care field say that they do it...care planning of itself is simple. It is the implementation of it that is the true challenge. (Foreword to Coleman *et al.* 1999)

NATIONAL MINIMUM STANDARDS

Standard 7

7.1   A service user plan of care generated from a comprehensive assessment is drawn up with each service user and provides the basis for the care to be delivered.

7.2   The service user's plan sets out in detail the action which needs to be taken by care staff to ensure that all aspects of the health, personal and social need of the service user are met. (DH 2002, p.9)

In all the years I have worked in social care I have seen many care plans and the information they have contained has varied tremendously. With the introduction of the new Care Standards Act 2000 one would hope that there will be more consistency in care planning. Sometimes the attitude of staff can present a problem. If a care worker has worked in an establishment for a very long time, s/he may be resistant to new ways of working: 'I have done care for the past 20 years. You can't teach me anything.' But care planning is not just about the actual practice of providing care; you cannot just 'do it'. Care workers have to be trained to:

- observe

- assess

- discuss

- liaise

- plan

- monitor

- review

- keep written records.

Handout 5.1, p.153

Nowadays great emphasis is placed on the importance of paperwork which must be undertaken as part of a care worker's job. Many people have a fear of having to write and struggle with literacy; this issue will be addressed further in Chapter 8. Consequently, some care plans may have been very sketchy in the past, whereas now it is expected that care plans should be very detailed. Someone like an Inspection Officer from the National Care Standards Commission should be able to pick up a care plan and know exactly what work is being undertaken with a service user and obtain a clear understanding of how the service user is living their life in the home or what resources are being provided in the day centre. A care plan should show how a service user is being cared for on a day to day basis.

Principles of care planning

In 1999 Counsel and Care produced the findings of a study which aimed 'to demonstrate that care and planning are not incompatible' (Coleman *et al.* 1999, p.1). The researchers 'identified and visited nine homes in a variety of locations and operating under varied management styles' and as a result identified seven central principles of care planning:

- Planning is about achieving and managing change, not just minding people.

- Bringing about change requires the setting of objectives, not just muddling through.

- Reaching objectives demands the preparation of strategies, not just waiting for things to happen.

- Preparing strategies needs information, not just guesswork.

- Handling information properly can only be done with good systems and accurate records, not just with impressions.

- Helping a person to change involves respecting all aspects of their life, not just isolated bits.

- Achieving and managing change, setting objectives, providing multi-dimensional care, preparing strategies, and assembling and storing information are tasks for teams not individuals, and teamwork rarely occurs without organisation. (Coleman *et al.* 1999, pp.10–11)

Meeting needs

The previous chapter was concerned with looking at the needs of older people, so when thinking about care planning the reader should revisit that chapter. Care planning is about meeting both the health and social care needs of the service user. Many service users will have been assessed by a social worker under the NHS and Community Care Act 1990. Practitioner guidance states:

Need is a multi-faceted concept which, for the purpose of this guidance, is sub-divided into six broad categories, each of which should be covered in a comprehensive assessment of need:

- Personal/social care

- Health care

- Accommodation

- Finance

- Education/employment/leisure

- Transport/access. (DH 1991, pp.12–13)

In previous chapters there has been an emphasis on being clear about definitions and terminology; this also applies to the term 'care planning'. It might have a slightly different meaning depending on what job a care worker is doing. So a little bit of history might help.

The NHS and Community Care Act 1990 brought in the system of Care Management which was defined as:

...the process of tailoring services to individual needs. Assessment is an integral part of care management but it is only one of seven core tasks that make up the whole process... (DH 1991, p.9)

The process had seven stages:

1. publishing information

2. determining the level of assessment

3. assessing need

4. care planning

5. implementing the care plan

6. monitoring

7. reviewing. (DH 1991, p.10)

Care planning was defined as:

> To identify the most appropriate ways of achieving the objectives identified by the assessment of need and incorporate them into an individual care plan. (DH 1991, p.61)

A service user could receive services while living in the community (hence the term 'Care in the Community'). What is relevant to the reader of this manual is that an older person may be receiving day care or respite care. On the other hand, after an assessment an older person may be admitted to a home. Therefore, care plans which are developed could be very different. Department of Health guidance states:

> 4.3   Care plans will vary according to the complexity of need. If it is a simple need which can be met by a single service, the care planning can be very swiftly accomplished. **All users in receipt of continuing service should have a care plan**, even if only a very brief one, which defines the user's needs and the objectives to be met by any service provided.

> 4.4   At the other extreme, care plans may be very complex, involving the co-ordination of services from a number of different agencies. The earlier that practitioners responsible for care planning are able to identify the contributing agencies and individuals the better they will be able to effect this co-ordination. (DH 1991, p.61)

Further on the guidance explains what should be recorded in a care plan:

> Care plans should be set out in concise written form, linked with the assessment of need. The document should be accessible to the user, for example, in braille or trans-

lated into the user's own language. A copy should be given to the user but it should also, subject to the constraints of confidentiality, be shared with other contributors to the plan. The compilation and distribution of such records has implications for the necessary levels of administrative support... A care plan should contain the following:

- the overall objectives
- the specific objectives of:
  - users
  - carers
  - service providers
- the criteria for measuring the achievement of these objectives
- the services to be provided by which personnel/agency
- the cost to the user and the contributing agencies
- the other options considered
- any point of difference between the user, carer, care planning practitioner or other agency
- any unmet needs with reasons – to be separately notified to the service planning system
- the named person(s) responsible for implementing, monitoring and reviewing the care plan
- the date of the first planned review. (DH 1991, p.67)

All the above will be relevant to care workers whether working in a home or day centre because they will have to read care plans written by social workers. Although care plans developed for use in a home or day centre may be slightly different, a lot can be learnt from the guidance mentioned above from the Department of Health. It is also important to be aware of changes which are being introduced regarding assessment; in the future Single Assessment will come into place. To keep up to date it is useful to access the Department of Health website: www.doh.gov.uk.

Care planning – the process

Good care planning will take time – it should not be rushed. A care worker must get to know a service user in order to understand them and identify their needs. The service user is central to the care plan. Keyworker sessions should be used to discuss and develop the care plan. In a day centre, a care worker should make time specifically to develop a care plan with the service user; that worker will have a similar role to a keyworker, but may not be known as such.

The role of the keyworker was discussed in Chapter 3; therefore, it will suffice to say here that the keyworker will play a major part in developing the care plan in conjunction with other people who will be mentioned below. In order to be able to write a detailed care plan the keyworker will need to engage the service user by showing genuine interest in them. It is not just about sitting and talking; much can be learnt about the service user and his/her past life as well as the present by using a variety of creative ways of working, such as:

- reminiscence

- lifestory work

- writing

- visits/outings.

Keyworker sessions should not be conducted in a public area. A service user is unlikely to talk about private matters if other people are around. In a home there will be private areas such as the service user's bedroom or small lounges which can be used for private meetings. In a day centre space might be more of a problem. However, privacy is of paramount importance.

Other people who may also be able to contribute to the care plan include:

- staff in home/day centre

- family

- friends

- professionals/workers

- advocates

- volunteers.

Handouts 5.2, 5.3 and 5.4 summarise key points for good practice in undertaking care planning. Exercise 5.1 will help care workers to think more broadly about which professional people might be able to contribute to a care plan. One should not forget or undervalue the contribution which could be made by workers in other organisations (for example in the private or voluntary sectors).

If a service user is perfectly mentally sound, then permission should always be sought before contacting people. However, if a service user does not have full mental capacity other people who have known that person previously may have very useful information; these could be professionals or family members. Family members or friends may be able to tell staff what a service user was like before s/he became confused – what that person liked or disliked. Once needs have been identified it has to be decided how they will be met; that is, objectives and methods of working must be recorded. Good recording skills are addressed in detail in Chapter 8, but it is necessary to emphasise here that care plans should be clear and detailed. If a care worker struggles with recording, it is important to encourage them to write in short, simple sentences in order to get the information across.

Once a care plan is written, it should be shared with the service user and then placed in his/her file in a safe place (usually in a filing cabinet in the office). However, that is only the beginning. Care plans need to be monitored and reviewed regularly; no one's life remains static.

NATIONAL MINIMUM STANDARDS

7.4   The service user's plan is reviewed by care staff in the home at least once a month, updated to reflect changing needs and current objectives for health and personal care, and actioned. (DH 2002, p.9)

What a care plan should include

Reference was made earlier to what was required in a care plan which is developed after an assessment by a professional. It is now important to turn attention to individual care plans which will developed specifically in a home or day centre. Most organisations will have developed their own format for care plans. However, the following is a summary of essential subject areas which should be included:

- basic personal details
- contacts, e.g. next of kin, other important people
- professionals, e.g. GP, speech therapist, physiotherapist
- other services, e.g. hairdresser

- needs

- levels of care/assistance required

- medical history

- health – physical and mental

- abilities/daily living

- relationships

- social history

- key events/important dates

- leisure/hobbies/interests

- personal values

- likes/dislikes

- death and dying

- objectives/methods of working

- risk assessment.

Handout 5.5, p.157

The care plan format should be designed so that it deals with every aspect of the service user's life. The importance of treating every service user as an individual was discussed at length in Chapter 2; this is another reason why service users have individual care plans and there should be flexibility in the format to address this. Every service user will present different needs and certain aspects of life might be more important to one person than to another.

How to develop a care plan

A new care worker who is going to be involved in developing care plans may feel at a loss for where to start. The importance of building up a relationship and developing trust has been emphasised and a care worker should have the social skills to do this. However, having basic questions to ask oneself is a good starting point for any care worker, experienced or not. A useful process is to break down the subject areas into sections and develop simple, straightforward questions. It will be helpful to consider an example.

Case Example: Personal care

Question: Does the service user need help with:

1. eating?

2. drinking?

3. toileting?

4. getting into/out of bed?

5. washing?

6. brushing teeth?

7. bathing?

8. showering?

9. washing hair?

10. brushing hair?

11. choosing what to wear?

12. dressing?

13. undressing?

14. taking medication?

Once a need has been identified a care worker has to think how it can be met. Again it is helpful to keep things simple by asking a question. The first example given below is about maintaining independence. Dependency levels in many homes will be high and some service users may be able to do very little for themselves. However, a service user should be encouraged to do even the smallest task; this will help them to maintain some independence and self-respect. Asking a question and having a checklist is a systematic way of getting a care worker to think about what the service user might be able to achieve. The checklist should include things that the service user may have done in the past. I am not suggesting that a care worker sits with the service user and goes through the checklist, but rather develops questions and checklists in preparation for a keyworker session.

Case Example: Maintaining independence

Question: Would the service user be able to:

1. tidy room?

2. make bed?

3. hoover?

4. clean?

5. wash up?

6. prepare drinks?

7. prepare snacks?

8. wash clothes?

9. iron?

10. look after a pet?

11. manage money?

12. use telephone?

13. write letter?

The following example is concerned with maintaining leisure and social interests.

Case Example: Social activities

Question: Would the service user be able to:

1. have relationships with other service users?

2. maintain relationships outside of the home with friends/family?

3. maintain previous interests/hobbies?

4. visit church, mosque etc?

5. smoke?

6. drink?

7. participate in games/activities provided by the home or day centre?

8. participate in physical exercise?

Very rarely is enough time spent finding out about a service user's hobbies and interests. Care workers must remember that they should be promoting the principle of fulfilment. Service users may have ambitions and hopes for the future; perhaps they want to attempt to do something out of the ordinary.

Case Example

Madge had been admitted to residential care because of her physical disabilities. She had a very active mind and had always enjoyed reading novels and plays. She told her keyworker that she had always wanted to get an 'A' level. There was a local community centre down the road from the home which ran further education classes some afternoons and evenings. In the summer months, the keyworker got a timetable for the following Autumn term. Madge registered for English Literature 'A' level. She attended every Tuesday afternoon and two years later she succeeded in getting her 'A' level.

Day care workers can develop the same method for developing care plans in their centre. A key part of their work may be in developing or maintaining skills so that a service user can remain living in the community.

Case Example: Going out

Question: Would the service user be able to:

1. use public transport?

2. go out for walks?

3. cross roads?

4. shop?

5. use public facilities, e.g. pub, library, cinema, leisure centre?

Matters regarding the health of the service user are of paramount importance. Homes and day centres need to know about health problems/medical conditions and medication which needs to be administered. All this should be written in the care plan. However, there will be times when a care worker may need to take advice from medical or nursing personnel because they do not have the expertise. There are so many conditions, diseases and types of medication that it is imperative to get the correct information so that mistakes are not made. There are many useful organisations that produce information leaflets about health matters (see Appendix 2). The following list summarises the basic information which a care worker needs to get and incorporate into a care plan:

- health problems (physical) – particular diseases, conditions

- mental health

- medication taken

- dietary problems (e.g. is there a need for a special diet?)

- hearing

- eyesight

- teeth

- feet

- continence

- medical personnel involved (e.g. GP, consultants, district nurse, community psychiatric nurse, speech therapist, physiotherapist)

- attendance at hospitals (e.g. is the service user currently attending an out-patient department?)

- specialist counsellors/therapists involved.

Case Studies 5.1, 5.2 and 5.3 may help care workers to think about how they would approach a service user and work with them in order to obtain information and develop a care plan.

Once care workers start thinking about writing care plans in a training session, some who are more experienced may realise that current care plans could be improved upon. Exercise 5.2 can be used to rewrite care plans or prepare for a review.

Layout of a care plan

It has already been said that many organisations will have a standard format for care plans, usually a form or a compilation of forms within a file. Whatever the format it needs to be one which encourages care workers to set clear objectives within achievable timescales. Therefore, organisations should provide written guidance and training on how to develop and write care plans.

Many care plans I see are badly designed. The space allocated for some subject areas is far too small and not every care worker realises that sheets of paper can be added if there is insufficient space to get everything down. It has been stressed that care plans need to be detailed so people understand what is being done to meet the needs of a service user. It is useful to have a summary sheet which covers the following points and can be used to review the care plan:

- objectives (what is going to be achieved within set time limits)
- how they will be achieved (state main methods of working)
- any changes in the service user or his/her circumstances since last review
- achievements
- difficulties in implementing the care plan
- things which need to be dealt with
- things which need to be changed.

Handout 5.6, p.158

Review

A care plan should not be written in tablets of stone. It needs to be reviewed because very rarely do situations remain static. The service user will experience changes, incidents, events in their life. All this will be recorded on the service user's file, but some major changes may affect the care plan; that is, some parts of it may need to be rewritten.

When the health of a service user who is living in a home deteriorates, there may be a need for a reassessment with a view to engaging a new service/resource or perhaps transferring from a residential home to a nursing home. The deterioration in health will have been monitored and there may have been adjustments to the care plan which show clearly how health needs have changed.

Case Example

Sally, who had been Grace's keyworker for the past six months, was getting very concerned about Grace and the fact that she was spending most of the day sitting in a chair in the lounge. Sally was sure that Grace had not been so lethargic when she had first got to know her, but could not pinpoint when things had begun to change. She decided to read back through Grace's file. Grace had been in the home for three years; the current and previous care plans were in the file. She had needed minimal help with personal care on admission, but had bouts of severe depression. A community psychiatric nurse had been involved. The care plans did not change much until nine months ago. Grace started refusing to be involved in the activities she normally liked. She started asking for help with dressing and bathing whereas she had always been determined to do everything she could herself. By reading back through the file it was clear just how much change there had been in the three-year period. It occurred to Sally that Grace may be suffering with depression and that some specialist help may be needed again.

Reading and storing care plans

To summarise, a care worker should be working in partnership with the service user and others to produce a detailed care plan, which is then monitored and reviewed regularly. When the care plan has been written it should be shared with the service user for their comments and amendments should be made if necessary. At this point the care worker should remind the service user about access and confidentiality. The service user can read the file at any time. If information needs to shared with anyone this would be discussed with the service user before doing anything.

The care plan must be stored in a safe place; this is usually in the service user's file, which is kept in a locked filing cabinet. Again it is important to emphasise that this should be explained clearly to the service user; it should not be assumed that a service user will know where the records are actually kept. It can be helpful (and more meaningful) to show service users around the office rather than just telling them where things are kept. This is equally important for service users attending a day centre.

Suggested reading

Bornat, J. (ed) (1994) *Reminiscence Reviewed: Perspectives, Evaluations, Achievements.* Buckingham: Open University Press.

Coleman, V., Regan, D. and Smith, J. (1999) *Who Care Plans.* London: Counsel and Care.

Gibson, F. (1998) *Reminiscence and Recall.* 2nd Edition. London: Age Concern.

Mallinson, I. (1996) *Care Planning in Residential Care for Older People in Scotland.* Aldershot: Avebury.

Murphy, C.J. (1994) *'It Started with a Sea-Shell': Life Story Work and People with Dementia.* Stirling: Dementia Services Development Centre.

Useful website

Department of Health: www.doh.gov.uk

📷 VIDEOS

Role of the Care Worker

Needs of the Service User

THINK OF A PROFESSIONAL/WORKER

Objective

To get care workers to think more creatively about which professionals/workers could contribute to a care plan.

Participants

This exercise can be done by an individual or in small groups.

Equipment

Paper and pen for the individual.
Flipchart paper and pens for groups.

Time

15 minutes.

Task

Make a list which includes any professional or worker from another organisation who may be able to give information or contribute directly to a care plan.

Feedback

Individuals will feed back to manager; groups will feed back to large group.

Note for trainer

Encourage participants to think broadly, not just in terms of who traditionally might be involved in a care plan. If they think creatively enough, they should be listing professionals like solicitors, bank managers, religious leaders etc. and workers from voluntary organisations or community groups.

THINK OF A SERVICE USER

Objective

To get care workers to rewrite care plans or prepare for a review.

Participants

Work on an individual basis.

Equipment

Paper and pens.
Access to care plans.
Copies of Handouts 5.1 to 5.6.

Time

30 minutes initially to plan what work needs to be undertaken in the future; the rewriting of the current care plan will take different lengths of time depending on the work needing to be done.

Task

1. Think of a service user you are currently involved with and for whom you have developed a care plan.

2. Read through the current care plan.

3. Read through Handouts 5.1 to 5.6.

4. Make a list of subject areas which have not been addressed adequately in the current care plan.

5. Are there other areas you think should be included?

6. Make a list of things you would like to discuss further with the service user.

7. Do you need to contact other people/organisations for more information? If so, who?

8. Is there any part of the care plan you could rewrite immediately?

Feedback

To line manager.

TASKS IN CARE PLANNING

- Observe

- Assess

- Discuss

- Liaise

- Plan

- Monitor

- Review

- Keep written records

CARE PLANNING SHOULD BE:

- Given thought

- Discussed with service user

- Discussed with other people who could be involved in providing care/a service

- Monitored

- Reviewed

WHO CAN CONTRIBUTE TO A CARE PLAN

- Service user

- Staff in home/day centre

- Family

- Friends

- Professionals/workers

- Advocates

- Volunteers

WHAT YOU CAN DO TO DEVELOP A CARE PLAN

- Ask the service user questions

- Make notes

- Ask people who know the service user questions

- Telephone people for information

- Contact specialist organisations

- Collect/file information

- Create a resource file

- Share information you obtain with the service user

SUBJECT AREAS TO BE COVERED IN A CARE PLAN

- Basic personal details

- Contacts, e.g. next of kin, other important people

- Professionals, e.g. GP, speech therapist, physiotherapist

- Other services, e.g. hairdresser

- Needs

- Levels of care/assistance required

- Medical history

- Health – physical and mental

- Abilities/daily living

- Relationships

- Social history

- Key events/important dates

- Leisure/hobbies/interests

- Personal values

- Likes/dislikes

- Death and dying

- Objectives/methods of working

- Risk assessment

CHECKLIST FOR PLANNING TO REVIEW A CARE PLAN

- Objectives (what is going to be achieved within set time limits)

- How they will be achieved (state main methods of working)

- Any changes in the service user or his/her circumstances since last review

- Achievements

- Difficulties in implementing the care plan

- Things which need to be dealt with

- Things which need to be changed

Case Study 5.1

Nancy is a 72-year-old Jewish woman, who has just been admitted to residential care. You have read the assessment which was written by the social worker and have taken in the basic information. Since being widowed at the age of 40, Nancy has spent a lot of time living on the streets. She has had an alcohol problem, been into several dry houses and has developed Korsakoff's syndrome. It has been assumed that she has no friends or relatives. Nancy keeps herself to herself; she does not like talking to other service users or staff. She has refused to have a bath and other service users are complaining about her personal hygiene.

Discuss

1. Having read this small amount of information, what questions are going through your head?

2. You have been told you are going to be Nancy's keyworker. What sort of things might you ask her during your first meeting with her?

3. What information will you need to acquire from Nancy in subsequent sessions?

4. Think about Nancy's identity and past history. Do you think you might be lacking in knowledge about some subject areas? If so, what exactly do you want to know and where would you go to find out more information?

Case Study 5.2

Gerald is 82 years old and has had several strokes, the last one leaving him without speech and the use of his right side. He is currently communicating by nodding and shaking his head and using hand signals. He has been admitted to a home, where he is visited regularly by all his children. Gerald has been married twice; he has four children from his first marriage who do not speak to the four stepchildren from his second marriage. Both his wives are dead. Talking to the relatives is very important for staff to gain information, but the children tell you very different things about Gerald's lifestyle, likes and dislikes. For example, his natural children say that Gerald is a practising Catholic and he needs to see the priest regularly. The stepchildren are Protestants and say Gerald gave up Catholicism when he married their mother.

Discuss

1. How are you going to communicate with Gerald now?
2. What suggestions can you make about using other methods of communication?
3. What are the main considerations for the care plan at the moment?
4. Which professionals might be involved with Gerald already?
5. Who do you need to talk to in order to clarify information?

Case Study 5.3

It is Mrs Wong's first day at day centre. Mrs Wong is 65 years old and came to live in England a year ago having lived in Hong Kong most of her life. After her husband died she wanted to be near her youngest son and his family. Since moving here she has suffered ill-health. She has had two admissions to hospital when her family thought she was having a heart attack; she has since been diagnosed as having angina. Mrs Wong has three grandchildren all under the age of five years; her daughter-in-law finds it hard to cope and so Mrs Wong has agreed to attend the day centre twice a week. The information which has been sent by the social worker to the day centre is rather scant. There is reference to the fact that Mrs Wong's son told the social worker his mother came to England because of financial problems. Mrs Wong can speak some English but at home she prefers to talk in Cantonese.

Discuss

1. You have been asked to welcome Mrs Wong as she arrives at day centre and help her to settle in. Is there anything you would want to find out before she arrived?

2. What would you need to ask Mrs Wong when she first arrived at the day centre?

3. What aspects of care planning would you need to consider?

4. Over the next few weeks what issues/subject areas would you raise and discuss with Mrs Wong?

Chapter 6
Risk Assessment

In recent years more emphasis has been put on the importance of undertaking risk assessments. This came about because of the increase in concern about public protection in the mid-1990s. However, the concept of risk is nothing really new – especially in the field of social care. For many years, social workers have referred to someone being 'at risk' and this term has also been used frequently by residential and day care staff. One theory of risk was developed over 20 years ago by Paul Brearley (1982a, 1982b) and is widely used by various organisations to develop their policies on risk assessment and risk management. Now that litigation is on the increase in this country, it is very important that organisations develop and implement effective risk policies, so that staff can demonstrate *how* they are minimising risk. The focus of this chapter will be on how to undertake thorough risk assessments based on Brearley's model of risk.

Risk is a part of life

We all take risks every day of our lives. Many of them we do not even think about – like getting into the car and driving on busy roads. More thought might be given to what are considered 'more serious' risks which may have serious implications; for example, major life changes: getting married, moving house, changing jobs.

Everyone should be able to live their lives as they wish to. People are very good at telling us what we should do and most of us have probably ignored sound advice because we think we know better or we have just been determined to do something anyway. It is important to remember this when working with service users. It is all too easy for care workers and professionals to become over-protective. Risk policies will usually make a clear statement about supporting risk-taking, an example being:

> The Council will fully support staff in enabling service users to exercise their rights to the full. The Council will support and accept responsibility for decisions taken by staff who have acted professionally and followed Departmental policies and procedures, even when harm results. (Rochdale Metropolitan Borough Council 2000, p.2)

However, the reality is that workers are often scared of the consequences, especially in the light of the increase in litigation already mentioned.

It is necessary to go back to the principles of care discussed in Chapter 2, especially in terms of individuality and respect. If a service user wishes to take risks in their life then they should be encouraged and supported to do so; they should not be discriminated against because of their age: 'You can't do that, you're too old.'

Undertaking a risk assessment is never easy, even when a service user is perfectly mentally sound and can make an informed decision. It becomes more complex and worrying when a service user does not have full mental capacity. The role of care workers is to help vulnerable people to understand the possible consequences of their actions. There can be many conflicts in risk assessment and care workers may feel that they are having to juggle too many balls in the air. This is because they are required to balance several things: benefits with possible harms; the wishes of the service user and the organisation's responsibilities. In some cases, it may be necessary to seek legal advice where the risk is deemed to be high. All this will be discussed in more detail below.

Care workers will be assessing all types of risk because service users engage in so many different types of activities: personal care; domestic tasks; community and social activities. A service user may not see 'what all the fuss is about'. Something they have done all their life is now being assessed; for example, walking to the toilet. It can be hard for an older person to accept that they may be at risk of harm, even when undertaking very simple tasks. Risk assessment must incorporate everybody's views; the perception of risk will vary from person to person. The service user may think there is no risk at all, whereas care staff may see that the possibility of harm occurring is high.

Exercise 6.1 will focus care workers on what they might think is unacceptable risk-taking. It will help them to reflect back on their own practice and consider whether they have encouraged or prohibited risk-taking.

The organisation's responsibility

Every organisation should have a risk policy in place which clearly states the fundamental principles in risk assessment and risk management. Lawson (1996) has stated there is a need for a risk policy to be in place if staff are to:

- make sound risk decisions

- feel good about the decisions they have made

- fully understand and articulate why they have made specific decisions. (Lawson 1996, p.51)

It should state clearly that if staff follow the policy then the organisation will support them should their practice be questioned. Writing a policy is not enough on its own; the organisation should ensure that:

- a clear procedure is written in conjunction with the policy; that is, offering clear guidance on what is expected of care workers

- training is offered on *how* to assess and manage risk.

In the work I do I very often see that risk assessment is skimmed over; in-depth training is needed so that workers realise how important this task is. They should have the time to think about risk-taking and develop an understanding of the theory. A crucial part of risk assessment is gathering information which may involve liaising with other people. It is only after this process has been undertaken that the risk assessment can be written. Care workers need time to practise writing risk assessments and developing the consequent care plans.

Management should not set the precedent that risk assessments can be done quickly. Obviously some risks are greater than others and the assessment will involve a much lengthier process. I am frequently told on training courses by staff: 'We haven't got time to do this.' Staff are regularly assessing risk as part of their day to day work, but in many cases they are not formalising the process and are therefore putting themselves at risk.

What is risk?

If care workers participate in Exercise 6.1 they will have come up with a list of risks they commonly deal with in their working lives. It will be useful at this point to be clear about terminology, which is often used incorrectly. Workers need to be clear about the following terms:

- risk-taking

- benefits

- hazards

- dangers.

The objective in undertaking a risk assessment is to assess whether a service user is likely to come to harm if s/he takes the risk – remembering that harm can be physical or emotional.

Definition Of Risk Assessment

The process of establishing whether or not someone is likely to seriously harm him/herself or others.

Risk-taking

To understand risk theory it is helpful to think in very simple terms. It is helpful if care workers ask themselves some very simple questions – What does the service user want to do? What is the service user doing which is causing staff concern? Risk-taking is the action; that is, the 'doing' word.

Benefits

Everyone takes a risk because they think they will get something out of it. For example, you may go on a roller coaster ride because of the feeling of excitement you get out of it; you may have that extra glass of wine because you think it is going to make you feel a bit merrier! It is necessary to find out from the service user why they want to do the action; that is, take the risk.

Hazards

A hazard can be anything – a person, an object, a condition; it can stop the service user getting any benefit or it may cause the actual danger(s).

Dangers

A danger is the worst feared outcome; that is, the harm (physical and emotional). It is important to list *all* the possible dangers. This will include harm to:

- the service user
- other people, i.e. the public – this will include other service users, staff, professionals, visitors to the home/day centre, people outside the home/day centre
- property, e.g. if a service user is violent, furniture or windows may be broken; a service user who smokes in bed may set light to the bedding, carpet etc.

Handout 6.1, p.181

Risk assessment and risk management have become more important in recent years because of the emphasis on promoting public protection and the fear of litigation.

Definition Of Public Protection

The protection of potential victims – it is the desired outcome of risk assessment and risk management.

The simple examples which follow will illustrate how the terms above are used and make care workers realise if they currently use terms incorrectly. A proper risk assessment would be written in more detail; this is just an outline to illustrate the point about correct use of terminology.

Case Example 1 – Ellen is a service user in a home

Risk-taking

Ellen wants to take a bath on her own.

Benefits

1. She feels she is independent.

2. She maintains her privacy and dignity.

Hazards

1. Ellen has severe arthritis.

2. Poor mobility.

3. Ellen is becoming slightly forgetful.

Dangers

1. Falling.

2. Sustaining injuries.

3. Death.

Case Example 2 – George attends day centre twice a week

Risk-taking

George wants to go to the local shops to buy a newspaper and cigarettes because he has no shops near him at home.

Benefits

1. He can get the things he needs on a regular basis.

Hazards

1. George is deaf.

2. He is partially sighted.

3. The shops are located across a dual carriageway.

4. Heavy traffic on a main road.

Dangers

1. Being run over.

2. Injuries.

3. Death.

Case Example 3 – Joan is a service user in a home

Risk-taking

Joan wants to eat large amounts of chocolate, sweets and puddings.

Benefits

1. She enjoys sweet things.

Hazards

1. Joan is already overweight – she currently weighs 16 stone.

2. She has a heart condition and has already had one heart attack.

3. She does not take any exercise at all and spends most of the time sitting watching the television.

Dangers

1. She will continue to put on weight.

2. Her health will deteriorate.

3. She will have another heart attack.

4. Death.

Case Example 4 – Fred attends a day centre

Risk-taking

Fred wants to go on the day centre trip to Scarborough.

Benefits

1. He does not get out socially, only to the day centre, so a trip out would be a treat.

2. He has always loved the seaside.

Hazards

1. Fred is wheelchair bound.

2. He has severe asthma attacks.

Dangers

1. Fred may have a severe asthma attack.

2. He may need medical attention.

Exercises 6.2 and 6.3 should help care workers to become clearer about terminology and how to write risk assessments. The following role-play exercise will also help them to prepare for interacting with a service to gain the necessary information for risk assessment.

☺ ROLE PLAY 6.1

Care workers will work in pairs. They will be given one of the case examples above. One care worker will role-play the care worker, the other will be the service user. The objective of the role play is for the care worker to talk to the service user about the risk-taking action and to gain information about the benefits to the service user. The care worker should also try to glean information about any possible hazards and the feared outcomes (dangers).

Principles of risk

A policy should clearly explain the fundamental principles of risk, which are:

1. *Self-determination*

    A service user should be able to live their life as they wish to do. S/he will be deemed capable of making an informed choice unless a formal assessment of mental capacity has indicated otherwise.

2. *Independence*

    A service user should be able to strive for and maintain as much independence as possible. Their activities or choices should not be restricted purely as a result of the concerns, anxieties and over-protectiveness of others.

3. *Service user focus*

    The risk assessment should focus primarily on the service user. His/her wishes and needs should not be over-ridden by the wishes of others.

4. *Equal opportunities*

    A risk assessment should take into consideration the background and needs of the service user and not discriminate on grounds of age, gender, religion, race, culture, sexuality or disability.

5. *Confidentiality*

    Confidentiality should be maintained in a risk assessment, but there will be occasions when information may have to be sought or shared. This could occur in situations where a service user does not have full mental capacity or it is agreed that the risk is so high it is in the person's best interests to break confidentiality.

6. *Staff support*

    An organisation's policy must state that staff will be supported if they follow the risk policy and procedural guidance.

Handout 6.2, p.182

The process

To do good risk assessments takes time; they should never be rushed or seen to be a paper exercise. The key stages are:

- get to know the service user
- talk about risk-taking

- liaise with other people (when appropriate)
- complete the risk assessment form
- convene a risk planning meeting
- predict likelihood of harm
- grade the level of risk
- develop the care plan
- set date for review.

Handout 6.3, p.183

Get to know the resident

Many risk assessments will have to be started as soon as a service user is admitted to a home or they start attending a day centre; at this stage it is not possible to get to know the person properly but a start can be made. Ideally a care worker should gain some understanding about the service user's lifestyle (now and in the past), their values and beliefs, and general philosophy of life. At the outset, the care worker should explain:

- why a risk assessment is being undertaken (purpose)
- what the risk assessment will entail (process)
- the importance of getting the service user's views (emphasising the principles of self-determination, independence, choice)
- the possibility of needing to gain other people's opinions (liaison)
- the boundaries of confidentiality/limits of information sharing (giving examples of when confidentiality may have to be broken).

Handout 6.4, p.184

Talk about risk-taking

A care worker will need to keep in mind the four terms – risk-taking, benefits, hazards and dangers. However, they need to speak in very straightforward language to a service user, so that the person does not become frightened that they are entering into some formal bureaucratic procedure. Having a normal conversation should draw out the required information if the right subject areas are introduced by the care worker.

Liaise with other people (when appropriate)

If the service user is perfectly mentally sound then it is necessary to ask permission to contact other people who might have an opinion about the risk-taking. If someone is confused or does not have full mental capacity for other reasons (e.g. brain damage, profound learning disabilities or dementia) then it may be necessary to over-ride the concept of self-determination. The care worker would discuss this with their line manager in the first instance. If other people were contacted for their opinion, staff in the home/day centre would be doing this because they felt they were acting in the person's best interests and they had the 'duty of care'. The reasons for doing this should be written very clearly in the service user's file and on the risk assessment form. People who might be contacted for their opinion might be:

- family/friends who know the person (these people might be particularly important in cases where the service user does not have full mental capacity and staff wish to know about what the person was like previously)

- professionals (e.g. social workers, GPs, district nurses, community psychiatric nurses, psychologists, psychiatrists, dieticians, physiotherapists, speech therapists)

- other people who might be involved with the service user (e.g. advocate, befriender).

When staff are unsure about a service user's mental state it is important to get a proper assessment of capacity (that is, not just asking someone 'What's today's date?' 'Who is the Queen?' 'Who is the Prime Minister?'). Different professionals can contribute to an assessment of mental capacity, but if for any reason capacity is being considered in a court of law the only person who can declare a person incapacitated is a psychiatrist. If a care worker is interested in learning more about capacity they should read guidance produced from the British Medical Association and Law Society (1995) and the Lord Chancellor's Department (1997, 1999, 2002); see website: www.lcd.gov.uk.

Complete the risk assessment form

A risk policy should include a risk assessment form. Many workers complain that there is not enough space in certain parts of the form. If a care worker needs to write more, s/he should know that it is acceptable to write on an A4 sheet of paper and attach it to the form. The form should be shared with the service user.

It is at this stage that a decision has to be made about whether to support the service user in taking the risk and how the risk of harm can be minimised. In many situations, having talked to the service user, a care worker may discuss the assessment with the manager of the home/day centre and other staff in order to develop a care plan. In cases where a service user might be deemed to be a high risk case a formal risk planning meeting might be convened.

Convene a risk planning meeting

If staff feel that the risk assessment should be discussed formally then the meeting should be chaired properly. Everyone who has contributed to the risk assessment or who may have an opinion about the risk-taking and its outcomes should be invited (this includes the service user) to the meeting. The chair of the meeting will use the risk assessment form as an agenda for the meeting.

Predicting risk and likelihood of harm

This is the hard bit of risk assessment. Brearley (1982b, p.13) stated there are two key questions to be asked:

1. What are the possible outcomes accessible in the state of current knowledge?

2. What is the probability that each of the possible outcomes will occur?

People who are involved in the risk assessment have to try to predict how likely it is that the *dangers* which have been listed are likely to occur. All the dangers should have been numbered; each one is discussed in turn by asking the question: '**How likely is this to occur?**' It is helpful to have a grading system on the risk assessment form, e.g.

- very likely

- quite likely

- unlikely

- not at all likely.

The discussion must focus on evidence produced. Evidence will be based on past behaviour/events and the current factors. Let us go back to Ellen in Case Example 1.

In order to assess if she is likely to fall when having a bath it would be necessary to have information about how often she has fallen during the past week, month and year.

For each danger written on the risk assessment form, there must be a consensus of opinion about likelihood and this should then be written on the form. Where there is a conflict of opinion, this should be noted in the *conflict box*, which should be present on the form. If it is not, the area of disagreement should be written up separately. Prediction is very subjective and this is what makes assessment so hard.

Grading the level of risk

Usually an organisation will have decided how risk is going to be graded; this will be explained in the policy and the scale shown on the risk assessment form. For example, the grade may range from 1 to 10 (1 being low, 10 being high) or 1 to 6. Otherwise, general terms may be used: low, moderate, high risk. Again a consensus of opinion needs to be reached regarding the grading of the overall risk-taking.

Develop the care plan

Having discussed all the dangers individually, the next question is: 'Is the service user going to be supported in taking the risk?' If the answer is positive, then the discussion focuses on *how* to support the service user. Methods of working need to be clearly written about how to minimise the risk of harm occurring. This is known as the *goal-setting* part of the process and will be written clearly into the care plan, which will include the following information:

- people to be involved, i.e. those who have actual tasks within the care plan – this may be staff in the home/day centre but also people outside (state name, relationship to service user, contact number)

- responsibilities (state area of responsibility and objectives for each person involved; be explicit about *who* is going to do *what* and *when*)

- how the care plan will be monitored (i.e. by whom and what tools will be used to record progress)

- where evidence will be recorded (this may include records from other workers/organisations)

- a date for review.

Handout 6.5, p.185

When the risk assessment has been completed, the form should be signed by *all* the people who agreed to the care plan. This will include:

- service user
- keyworker/other care workers who have a key role
- manager
- family members (if appropriate)
- professionals/workers (if appropriate).

Obtaining signatures on the risk assessment form is a key element of the risk assessment process because it ensures joint accountability. If someone disagrees with the decision, then this should be noted in the conflict box.

Set a date for review

Risk assessment is only the beginning; the next step is to manage risk. Very often risk policies do not give enough attention to this part of the process. It is very important at the time of completing a risk assessment that a date is set for review. This is the start of risk management.

Risk management

Risk management can be defined as action to monitor a person's behaviour and attitudes, and to intervene in his/her life, to try to prevent them seriously harming him/herself or others. Care workers will be managing risk every day of their working lives but it is important to remember that this needs to be formally monitored. Once a care plan is in place, the staff within a home or day centre will need to record any changes, successes and failures. It should not be assumed that once a risk assessment has been done that the care plan is automatically going to be successful. Sometimes the planned way of working is inappropriate, but it is only with testing it out that this becomes apparent.

Definition Of Risk Management

The action taken to monitor a person's behaviour and attitudes and to intervene in his/her life to try to prevent them seriously harming him/herself or others.

Suggested reading

Counsel and Care (1992) *What if They Hurt Themselves.* London: Counsel and Care.

Counsel and Care (1993) *The Right to Take Risks.* London: Counsel and Care.

Lawson, J. (1996) 'A Framework for Risk Assessment and Management for Older People.' In H. Kemshall and J. Pritchard (eds) *Good Practice in Risk Assessment and Risk Management.* London: Jessica Kingsley Publishers.

Littlechild, R. (1996) 'Risk and Older People.' In H. Kemshall and J. Pritchard (eds) *Good Practice in Risk Assessment and Risk Management.* London: Jessica Kingsley Publishers.

Pritchard, J. (1997) 'Vulnerable People Taking Risks: Older People and Residential Care.' In H. Kemshall and J. Pritchard (eds) *Good Practice in Risk Assessment and Risk Management 2: Protection, Rights and Responsibilities.* London: Jessica Kingsley Publishers.

Useful website

Lord Chancellor's Department: www.lcd.gov.uk

VIDEOS

Risk Assessment (Moving and Handling)

Risk Assessment (Health and Safety)

Managing Challenging Behaviour

ACCEPTABLE AND UNACCEPTABLE RISK-TAKING?

Objective

To get care workers to think about promoting risk-taking and to admit when they have stopped a service user doing something because of their age or disability.

Participants

Small groups.

Equipment

Flipchart paper.
3 different coloured pens.

Time

30 minutes.

Task

1. Make a list of the 'typical' risks you have to assess when working with service users in your home/day centre.

2. Add to the list any risks a service user has wanted to take but maybe has not been allowed to do.

3. When you have finished the list read through it again and discuss what is acceptable and unacceptable risk-taking.

4. Put a tick (✓) by the risks which are acceptable and a cross (✗) by what you consider to be unacceptable risks.

5. Write down the reasons why you think the risks marked with an ✗ are unacceptable.

Feedback

1. Each group will present their list of risks and the main points from their discussions.

2. Groups will comment on whether they agree or disagree with the risks which are said to be unacceptable.

3. The trainer will facilitate discussion about what makes risk-taking acceptable or unacceptable.

Note for trainer

Some participants who are new to risk assessment may have difficulty in grasping the concept of risk-taking. They may get confused between risk-taking and dangers. The trainer should be accessible to participants throughout this exercise in order to talk through any difficulties.

BENEFITS

Objective

To encourage care workers to see the benefits of risk-taking from the service user's point of view.

Participants

Small groups.

Equipment

Flipchart paper and pens.

Time

30 minutes.

Task

1. Look at the risk-taking actions which you found unacceptable in Exercise 6.1. List them on the left side of the flipchart sheet.

2. Try to consider why the service user might want to do these things.

3. List the possible benefits on the right hand side of the flipchart sheet.

Feedback

1. Each group will feed back the benefits discussed.

2. Large group discussion will focus on the reasons why the risks listed were thought to be unacceptable.

3. Participants will be asked to add to the list of benefits.

HAZARDS AND DANGERS

Objective

To help care workers develop a clear understanding about the difference between hazards and dangers.

Participants

Small groups.

Equipment

3 sheets of flipchart paper. Each sheet will have a heading: (i) risk taking, (ii) hazards, (iii) dangers. The trainer should prepare the sheets beforehand.
Coloured pens.

Time

30 minutes.

Task

1. Think about service users you work with. Discuss in your group the typical risk-taking actions you observe. List them on flipchart sheet (i).

2. For each risk-taking action listed on flipchart sheet (i) discuss the related hazards and list them on sheet (ii).

3. Finally, make a list of dangers on flipchart sheet (iii).

Feedback

1. The trainer will take feedback from groups by first going through the lists of (i) risk-taking actions followed by (ii) hazards and finally (iii) dangers.

2. The trainer will encourage groups to say if they think another group has written something on the wrong sheet i.e. a hazard should be a danger or vice versa.

3. Open discussion about differentiating between a hazard and a danger.

Note for trainer

Participants usually get very muddled up when undertaking this exercise. It is important for the trainer to visit each group regularly as they are working and correct them if they are going wrong.

BASIC QUESTIONS FOR RISK ASSESSMENT

RISK-TAKING

What does the service user want to do?

BENEFITS

What will the service user get out of taking the risk?

HAZARDS

What might stop the service user getting the benefits or cause the dangers?

DANGERS

What is the worst that can happen?

PRINCIPLES OF RISK

- Self-determination

- Independence

- Service user focus

- Equal opportunities

- Confidentiality

- Staff support

KEY STAGES OF RISK ASSESSMENT

- Get to know the service user

- Talk about risk-taking

- Liaise with other people (when appropriate)

- Complete the risk assessment form

- Convene a risk planning meeting

- Predict likelihood of harm

- Grade the level of risk

- Develop the care plan

- Set date for review

EXPLAINING RISK ASSESSMENT TO THE SERVICE USER

A care worker should take time to explain to a service user:

- Why a risk assessment is being undertaken (purpose)

- What the risk assessment will entail (process)

- The importance of getting the service user's views (emphasising the principles of self-determination, independence, choice)

- The possibility of needing to gain other people's opinions (liaison)

- The boundaries of confidentiality/limits of information sharing (giving examples of when confidentiality may have to be broken)

GOAL-SETTING IN RISK ASSESSMENT

The following information should be included in a care plan regarding goal-setting; that is, how steps will be taken to minimise risk.

- **People to be involved**
  i.e. those who have actual tasks within the care plan – this may be staff in the home/day centre but also people outside (state name, relationship to service user, contact number)

- **Responsibilities**
  (state area of responsibility and objectives for each person involved; be explicit about *who* is going to do *what* and *when*)

- **How the care plan will be monitored**
  (i.e. by whom and what tools will be used to record progress)

- **Where evidence will be recorded**
  (this may include records from other workers/organisations)

- **A date for review**

Chapter 7

Effective Communication

There is an emphasis throughout this manual that a care worker should be doing things *with* the service user rather than *to* them. In order to achieve this effective communication will be essential. It is not just about talking to a service user; there are numerous imaginative and creative ways to communicate, which will be the subject of this chapter. (Written communication will be addressed in the following chapter.)

Why we need to communicate

Even if a person enjoys their own company there will be times when s/he has to communicate; as the saying goes 'no man is an island'. A service user will need to communicate their needs and wishes to a care worker in order that a quality service can be provided. However, some service users may have difficulty in communicating – hence the reasons for a care worker to develop skills in both verbal and non-verbal communication.

Dictionary Definition

Communicate
Share or exchange information or ideas; pass on, transmit or convey.

What is communication?

Communication is about listening and responding. It can be:

- verbal

- non-verbal

- behavioural

- written.

Handout 7.1, p.208

Care workers must be trained to think how they communicate in all the above ways. Exercises need to be undertaken to improve both listening and responding skills. Michael Jacobs in *Swift to Hear* (1985), which is an excellent resource for exercises on developing listening and responding skills, summarises the guidelines for listening and responding as follows:

Guidelines for LISTENING

1. Listen with undivided attention, without interrupting.

2. Remember what has been said, including the details (the more you listen and the less you say, the better your memory).

3. Listen to the 'bass line' – what is not openly said, but possibly what is being felt.

4. Watch for non-verbal clues to help you understand feelings.

5. Listen to yourself, how you might feel in a described situation, as a way of further understanding – empathy.

6. Try to tolerate pauses and silences that are a little longer than usual in conversations (and avoid asking lots of questions to break silences).

7. Help yourself and the other to feel comfortable and relaxed with each other; keep calm even when you don't feel calm.

Guidelines for RESPONDING

8. Be as accurate as possible in describing feelings/ideas that you perceive (not just 'depressed' or 'angry').

9. Use your empathic understanding, again making this accurate, although also tentative (you may be wrong).

10. Keep questions to a minimum, unless:

    you need precise information (in which case ask precise questions);
    you want to open up an area (in which case use open-ended questions);
    you wish to prompt (when rhetorical questions help);
    and avoid at all costs questions beginning 'Why…?'

11. Use minimal prompts: 'mm', 'yes', or the last few words.

12. Paraphrase or reflect as accurately as:

    a way of prompting;
    an indication that you have been listening;
    a way of checking out that you have heard correctly.

13. Avoid making judgements or loaded remarks.

14. Where possible link reported experiences, events, reactions and ideas.

15. Avoid changing the subject or interrupting unnecessarily.

16. Avoid speaking too soon, too often, or for too long.

And finally, when you have responded:

17. Return to the listening mode, to watch and listen for the reaction to your own response, as well as anything new that emerges.

(Jacobs 1985, pp.13–14)

Who we communicate with

A care worker is going to have to communicate with a lot of different people in order to identify and meet the needs of service users. Chapter 4 showed just how many needs could be presented; therefore, it is important that a care worker has developed skills to understand the service user but also to be able to seek out information and help from other people.

It is easy to take for granted who we communicate with on a day to day basis when in the work situation, because we do not really give it much thought:

- service users
- family/friends of service users
- colleagues
- other people in the organisation
- professionals
- visitors to the home/day centre
- people in other agencies/organisations.

Neither do we think about *how* we communicate because it is something we probably think comes naturally. Exercise 7.1 can be used to encourage care workers to think about how they have communicated recently and with whom. We can all improve our communication skills in some way and Exercise 7.2 has been designed so that care workers can identify their strengths and weaknesses and set objectives to further develop effective communication skills.

When communicating with anyone, a care worker needs to think about a lot of different things which will become more apparent as this chapter is read. However, the main things which a care worker need to think about are:

- voice
- eye contact
- facial expressions

- position and use of body

- breathing.

Handout 7.2, p.209

Verbal communication

A care worker might have to use verbal communication in all sorts of different situations at work:

- talking face-to-face or on the telephone with service users, colleagues, family members, professionals

- presenting information in meetings/reviews

- during handovers

- having supervision

- attending training courses.

Because care workers usually spend a lot of time talking during the course of the day, a lot of them would probably say they were good at verbal communication. However, it is important to analyse *what* is actually said and done. Sometimes it is easier for us to learn from other people – they can give us insight into what we do. It may take some courage, but Exercise 7.2 can be repeated by asking a colleague to list what we are not very good at regarding verbal communication. They may say you:

- have an accent they find difficult to understand

- use words or sayings local to your area which they do not understand

- use jargon, cliches, trendy phrases

- talk too quickly or slowly

- talk too softly or loudly

- mumble

- sigh a lot.

A care worker may feel confident talking to a service user or a colleague, but there might be situations in which they feel nervous – perhaps having to participate in a review; having to talk to someone who is intimidating. These situations may affect how a care worker will talk – for example: voice goes high pitched or quiet; stammers; forget what is going to be said; cannot find the right words. If a care worker identifies that they need to improve their verbal skills then they need to be encouraged to practise in private but also in supervision sessions; that is, they need to rehearse. Key points to be remembered are:

- think before you speak
- be clear about what you are saying
- speak loud enough/not too loudly
- do not speak too fast
- think about the language you use.

Handout 7.3, p.210

In day to day work care workers are going to have to think on their feet a lot of the time, but when they might have to contribute to a meeting or gain information it is important to prepare. When someone is nervous, they might talk much quicker than they normally do. When talking to a group of people or to someone who has communication difficulties it is necessary to slow down; you may even sound to yourself that you are talking too slowly but you are probably talking at the right speed for others to understand you. It is vital to talk clearly and loud enough; there is nothing worse than someone asking you to repeat what you have just said – especially in a formal meeting!

Rehearsal in front of a mirror and recording oneself (e.g. using a dictaphone) can be a really good (if frightening) way of seeing and hearing how one presents oneself. Similarly, rehearsal can be carried out in supervision sessions or in practice sessions with a colleague. Role play is hated by many people but it is a useful way of practising for difficult encounters. By using these methods care workers can prepare themselves before actually engaging in verbal communication.

We all get nervous and may even panic when we are communicating with someone. If this happens, a care worker must think about breathing deeply from their lungs rather than shallowly from the chest. This is where pauses and silences can be useful; they give a care worker time to think what they are going to say next and restore some calm by taking deep breaths.

What is actually said is very important.

Key Question
Does the person understand what I am saying?

Care needs to be taken about the words used. In different parts of the country a word might have different meanings or there may be colloquialisms peculiar to a local area. Care workers need to ensure that they use politically correct language and do not talk in an oppressive or discriminating way.

Think about
WHAT is said and **HOW** it is said.

Expression – that is, *how* something is said – is important because a person will interpret what you mean by the way you say the words. The tone of voice may indicate a great deal, put together with body language, which will be discussed below. A care worker needs to reflect on how s/he uses the voice.

There are a lot of things to think about when using this tool:

- tone
- pitch
- inflection
- spacing of words
- use of emphases
- pauses
- silences.

Handout 7.4, p.211

The use of pauses and silences needs to be emphasised because it is very easy to finish sentences off for someone or jump in when there is a silence. Silences make many people feel uncomfortable and obligated to fill the gap. A care worker should learn to use the counting technique – when there is a silence count to five slowly before talking again. Some people just have the irritating habit of butting in or cutting across people anyway. If a care worker is under pressure then s/he might just rush the service user so they can get on with other work.

Task

Practise:
- speaking clearly
- not interrupting
- not rushing
- counting so you use pauses and silences correctly
- breathing deeply.

Questions, prompts and reflection

Some people are naturally nosey, others have what might be termed 'healthy curiosity'; these people are likely to ask a lot of questions, which is exactly what a care worker should not do. Obviously questions have to be asked, but if a service user has some communication difficulties it can be easy to fall into the trap of bombarding them with questions, or, as mentioned above, people may use questions to fill an awkward silence. A good technique is to try 'to get the person to tell their story' in their own words or own way. Hence the concept of the storyteller and the listener introduced in Exercise 7.3.

Conversation will come very naturally for most care staff, but situations will occur when it will be crucial that a care worker does not lead a service user; that is, put words in their mouth ('Did you go to bed at 10.00?') or manipulate them in to giving certain answers by the way a question is phrased (e.g. 'You *do* want to go to the toilet now, don't you?').

There are two types of question:

- **Closed questions** will get a 'yes' or 'no' response. ('Do you want to watch television?')

- **Open questions** will encourage the respondent to use their own words. ('What would you like to do now?')

Useful words to start sentences with are:

- How?

- Who?

- What

- When?

- Where?

'Why' is a word to be avoided, because it can put pressure on a service user to give an explanation or it can just be totally irritating. (Think of a small child you have known who continually asked 'why?'. Did you get annoyed?)

Handout 7.5, p.212

To avoid using too many questions, it can be useful to use the *reflection* technique. This is when the listener repeats the exact words used by the speaker but reflects it back as a question using inflection in the voice. Caution must be exercised in not using the reflection technique all the time – otherwise the service user may think you are not bothering to listen at all. Reflection can be used in conjunction with short prompts to encourage the service user to communicate more in their own words.

Case Example

Service user says: 'I feel really sad today.'
A care worker may be tempted to say: 'Why's that then?'
In order to avoid using 'why', **reflection** could be used:

'You feel sad today?'

Or the following **prompts/probes**:

'Tell me more.'

'What's making you feel that way?'

'When did this start?'

Non-verbal communication

At times body language can say more about what a person means than the words they are speaking; non-verbal clues may indicate how a person is feeling. A care worker needs to be mindful of their own body language and how they might be perceived by the service user or other people they communicate with, but there is also a need to be able to interpret body language. This could be especially important for service users who have no speech or some form of sensory impairment – they will be relying on body language to a greater degree.

Body language

Body language is important whether communication is verbal or non-verbal; it will also be relevant when considering behavioural communication. Again it is important to emphasise the need for care workers to analyse themselves; that is, to be aware of what their body does. We all have mannerisms which are peculiar to ourselves; some we are conscious of, others people may tell us about.

Before talking in depth about body language it is important to acknowledge that in some cultures body language may be very different. For example, it may be regarded as rude to maintain eye contact. If a care worker has to work with someone from a different ethnic background it is vital that information is sought on this topic.

When thinking about body language a care worker should also think about positioning; that is, one should never get too close to a person during communication. A good guide is that you should try to maintain about three feet between you and the person you are communicating with. Everyone needs their own personal space.

Some service users may need to see your mouth or your face clearly and therefore it is appropriate to sit or stand directly opposite the person in these circumstances. Otherwise, it is better not to assume a position which may be deemed confrontational; it is better to be at a slight angle.

A care worker needs to be aware of the whole body; it can often shift position without a person realising this. Examples are: if a person does not like what they are hearing or seeing, the body may turn away from the person who is speaking or doing the action; if a person is being defensive/protective they may cross their arms and legs.

Posture is important. It is good to adopt a relaxed, open position to facilitate communication. It feels very uncomfortable for most of us not to cross arms and legs, but it can be interpreted as a barrier to good communication. Care workers should practise the '5 minute body rule'.

Task – The 5 Minute Body Rule

When a care worker is engaged in a communication activity which is going to last for more than 30 minutes (e.g. they are going to be involved in a staff meeting, keyworker session, supervision session, training course) they have to check the position of their body every 5 minutes to gauge how it has changed, if at all.

Jerky or sudden movements can be disturbing or perceived as threatening to some people; for example, if they have a learning disability, are partially sighted or have dementia. We all have bad habits – perhaps fiddling with rings, hair, pens; jogging a foot; using hands too much when talking. It is important to make a conscious effort not to do these things when trying to communicate effectively; these habits can detract from what you are trying to convey.

Task – Identify and Work on Bad Habits

1. Make a list of all the bad body language habits you have.
2. Ask your colleagues if they have noticed any of your bad habits.
3. Ask your family members/friends the same question.

A care worker needs to be conscious of the different parts of the body:

- head
- facial expressions
- eye contact
- arms

- hands

- legs

- feet.

Handout 7.6. p.213

It is always difficult to know what your face is showing and an expression can easily be misinterpreted. You might be concentrating hard, but someone else might see you as frowning. Someone at a distance might see you laughing and think you are having a joke when the reality is you do not know how to react to a situation and you are responding with a nervous giggle. Good advice is just to think about what your face might be showing. No matter what a care worker is feeling inside, the following should never be shown:

- shock

- horror

- disgust

- upset.

How a person breathes can also tell you a lot about how they might be feeling. When someone is nervous, anxious, panicky or fearful, it is likely that they will breathe more quickly. This is a non-verbal clue. A care worker who is struggling with a situation and is unsure what to do should consciously try to breathe more slowly and deeply; as mentioned above this can done while using pauses and silences.

A care worker should use gestures to indicate that they are listening and to encourage the service user to continue communicating:

- nodding

- slight tilt of head to one side

- showing palm of hand upwards

- beckoning with one hand.

A worker should also be conscious of the fact that s/he may copy the body language of the person with whom they are communicating. This is known as mirroring. It can happen when a person is in agreement with the communicator or even if there is no agreement. For example, when a care worker is facing an aggressive service user s/he may start to mirror that physical aggression. This is dangerous practice and will be discussed further in Chapter 10.

The use of touch

The use of touch is a very difficult subject area. Touch is obviously a powerful way of communicating with somebody, but in the work situation it has to be used appropriately and sensitively; that is, it is imperative to keep within professional boundaries. A care worker should always ask themselves: 'How could my behaviour be viewed by someone else?' We are living in an era where we have to be very careful about everything we do in the work situation. Somebody could walk in and misinterpret your actions – how would an outsider see kissing, cuddling or holding hands with a service user?

> **Key Question**
>
> How could my behaviour be viewed by someone else?

Lots of people say that they are a 'touchy-feely' type person and they 'can't help it'. The point is that a care worker has to modify their actions if it is not appropriate in the work situation. Touch can be used in a positive way to encourage and reassure, but it must not be over-used. It has to be remembered that some people do not like being touched at all; there could be any number of reasons for this. The role of the care worker is to get to know a service user and find out when it is appropriate to use touch. Touch can be used to:

- reassure
- comfort
- encourage
- guide
- stop.

Handout 7.7, p.214

Barriers to communication

So far we have been talking about good practice in communication but we also need to look at when communication is hindered in some way; that is, there are difficulties or barriers. A service user could experience difficulty in communicating because s/he has:

- a different first language
- no speech
- lost hearing
- lost sight
- learning disabilities
- dementia
- mental health problems
- never learnt to read/write.

The care worker must find appropriate ways of communicating or enlist the help of someone else who can, e.g. interpret, use sign language, use a particular communication system/board. Lots of other things can hinder communication – perhaps a service user discriminates in some way (e.g. does not like men, a particular ethnic group, a care worker) and consequently refuses to communicate with certain people. The environment can also impede communication; for example, for service users with a sensory impairment, noise levels or lack of good lighting could make life difficult.

Case study 7.1, p.216

Behavioural changes

Moods affect how we act. When we are happy we talk and behave in a very different way to when we are sad or angry. We will act depending on how we feel. If someone's behaviour starts to change we should be asking what has happened to make it change. It could be a medical condition (physical or mental) which is causing the behavioural changes, but fundamental questions should be: 'What is the reason for this change in behaviour?' followed by 'What is the person trying to tell me?'

Good Practice Point

Do not label people. If a person's behaviour changes ask some simple questions:

What is the reason for this change in behaviour?

What is the person trying to tell me?

Dealing with challenging behaviours will be discussed in detail in Chapter 10. For now it will suffice to say that certain conditions will affect mental capacity and the ability to understand and hence communicate. For example, a person who is in the early stages of dementia might not understand certain words which are spoken to them. They may find this very frustrating and start to become very bad-tempered. Another person with dementia might start wandering around the home or day centre, where previously they have always sat for long periods of time.

Case study 7.2, p.217

The subject of self-harm can cause care workers anxiety; this is often due to lack of knowledge about this type of behaviour. Self-harm 'is an act which involves deliberately inflicting pain and/or injury to one's own body, but without suicidal intent' (Arnold and Babiker 1998, p.133). Injuries are usually superficial, but risk assessments must be undertaken if a service user regularly self-harms. Typical behaviours which may cause concern for care staff may be:

- cutting – commonly on arms and legs
- burning parts of the body
- banging parts of the body against something.

If a service user does self-harm, the role of a care worker will be to try to find out why s/he needs this form of release. This behaviour may be a reaction to something that happened in childhood or earlier in life – abuse, maltreatment, neglect, bereavement or loss. A care worker needs to gain some understanding about self-injurious behaviour before they can work effectively with a service user; this behaviour is a way of communicating for the service user.

Case study 7.3, p.218

Aids to communication

In this chapter a lot of attention has been given to how a human being can communicate and the personal resources we are equipped with – listening and responding skills, use of body language etc. But sometimes we will need other things to help us communicate in a better way; for example, specialised methods of working, equipment and aids.

A care worker needs to be trained to use creative methods of working with a service user to improve communication; for example:

- reminiscence work

- making a lifestory book

- using orientation/validation methods.

Older people may like to reminisce or undertake a formal life review; they may want to do this for different reasons, one of which may be that it is a way of telling a care worker about themselves and their current needs. A care worker can encourage a

Case Example

Jean had been diagnosed with a terminal illness and knew that she had about six months to live. She said she wanted to talk about her life and 'to be able to leave some legacy, but I have nothing'. Her keyworker, Lynne, suggested that they start to make a lifestory book which could be left to her children. Jean told her story to Lynne, who then wrote whatever Jean wanted in the book. Jean had some photographs herself, but also asked family members to bring in some of theirs so she could choose which ones were to be glued into the book. One of Jean's wishes was to visit the house where she had been born and go into the church where she had been married. These two visits were organised before she became very ill and could not get out of the home. Lynne took a camera with them on the visits, so photographs could be put into the book.

service user to reminisce by talking or by writing or drawing. A really interesting way of working is to help a service user make a lifestory book, which literally tells their life in words, pictures etc. It can also involve visits to important places.

There may be other professionals/therapists who can be brought in to help a service user communicate through:

- art
- drama
- music
- aromatherapy.

Practical aids may be needed to improve communication. We are living in an age where technological developments are making life easier for people who have communication difficulties:

- hearing aids
- loop systems
- adaptors
- microphone aids
- headphones
- doorbell/light flashes
- alarm clocks
- Makaton/communication boards
- electronic writing machines.

However, a care worker should not forget about simple things which can aid communication:

- signs
- pictures
- cards
- writing paper and pen.

Handout 7.8, p.215

Case study 7.4, p.219

☺ ROLE PLAY 7.1

Day care worker:

Vincent has just turned 65 years of age. He has some learning disabilities which affect the way in which he communicates. He can say some simple words, but gets the meaning wrong sometimes. For many years he has been attending a social education centre; the staff there were able to communicate very well with him and used symbols. Because of his age he has had to transfer to your day centre. Today you are going to try to get to know Vincent a little better. You are talking to him privately – away from the other service users.

Vincent:

You are a 65-year-old man with learning disabilities and have just started attending a day centre which you find very strange because for years you have attended the social education centre where everyone knew you really well and understood what you said. You speak slowly, use only simple words and get the meaning of words wrong (i.e. you use them incorrectly and misunderstand what people ask you). Today a day care worker is going to talk to you alone away from the other day centre users.

☺ ROLE PLAY 7.2

Participant 1 will be the service user:

Think of a service user in your workplace who has communication difficulties. You are going to role-play that person.

Participant 2 will be the care worker:

Before the role play begins ask your partner who s/he is and what sort of communication difficulties s/he has.

The care worker will initiate a conversation about what has happened in the past two days when she has been off.

Suggested reading

Arnold, L. and Babiker, G. (1998) 'Counselling People Who Self-Injure.' In Z. Bear (ed) *Good Practice in Counselling People Who Have Been Abused.* London: Jessica Kingsley Publishers.

Arnold, L. and Magill, A. (1996) *Working with Self-Injury: A Practical Guide.* Bristol: The Basement Project.

Gibson, F. (1998) *Reminiscence and Recall.* 2nd Edition. London: Age Concern.

Jacobs, M. (1985) *Swift to Hear.* London: SPCK.

Useful organisations

Change (works and campaigns for people with both a learning disability and a sensory impairment)

Block D Hatcham Mews Business Centre, Hatcham Park Mews, London SE14 5QA

Tel: 020 7639 4312 Fax: 020 7639 4317

E-mail: contact@changeuk.demon.co.uk Website: www.changepeople.co.uk

RNIB (Royal National Institute of the Blind)

105 Judd Street, London WC1H 9NE

Tel: 020 7388 1266 Fax: 020 7388 2034 Helpline: 0845 766 9999

E-mail: helpline@rnib.org.uk Website: www.rnib.org.uk

RNID (Royal National Institute for Deaf and Hard of Hearing People)

19–23 Featherstone Street, London EC1Y 8SL

Tel: 0808 808 0123 Textphone: 0808 808 9000 Fax: 020 7296 8199

E-mail: informationline@rnid.org.uk Website: www.rnid.org.uk

SENSE (for people who are deafblind or have associated disabilities)

11–13 Clifton Terrace, Finsbury Park, London N4 3SR

Tel: 020 7272 7774 Fax: 020 7272 6012

E-mail: enquiries@sense.org.uk Website: www.sense.org.uk

VIDEOS

Effective Communication 1

Other videos which will be relevant to this chapter are:

Role of the Care Worker

Needs of the Service User

Managing Challenging Behaviour

THE LAST SHIFT

Objective

To make care workers think about how they use different ways of communicating.

Participants

Individual work, then share in pairs.

Equipment

Paper and pens.

Time

10 minutes to make list; 10 minutes to share work.

Task

1.   Think about the last shift you worked and reflect back on what you did through that time.

2.   Make a list of people you communicated with.

3.   Make a list of ways in which you communicated with those people.

Feedback

Share your list with one other person.

WEAKNESSES AND STRENGTHS

Objective

To identify strengths and weaknesses in communication skills and to set targets to work on weaknesses identified.

Participants

Individual work, then joint work with manager.

Equipment

Paper and pens.

Time

15 minutes to make list; discussion in supervision session.

Task

1. Think about the four ways of communicating:

    - verbal
    - non-verbal
    - behavioural
    - written

    and how you use them in your work situation.

2. Make a list of what you are really good at for each type of communication.

3. Make a list of what you are bad at for each type of communication.

4. Share your list with your manager.

5. Develop an action plan on how you will work on improving your weaknesses.

Feedback

1. The action plan developed should be reviewed regularly by the care worker and manager in order to monitor the worker's development in communication skills.

Note for trainer

This exercise can be repeated by getting the care worker to ask someone else (e.g. a colleague) to do tasks 1 to 3, and then the list is shared with the care worker.

LISTENING, RESPONDING AND REFLECTION

Objective

To practise listening skills.

Participants

To work in pairs.

Equipment

Trainer to keep time.

Time

25 minutes.

Task

1. The pairs will decide who will be Number 1 and who will be Number 2.

2. Trainer will introduce the concept of the storyteller and the listener.

3. Participants will be asked to reflect for one minute on their last holiday, short break or day out.

4. Number 1 will be the designated storyteller. S/he will talk about their holiday for 5 minutes. Number 2, who will be the listener, can only use body language to communicate.

5. After 5 minutes, Number 2 will summarise what has been said by Number 1, but also how they perceived the storyteller's feelings.

6. The exercise is repeated with Number 2 as the storyteller (talking about their holiday) and Number 1 as the listener, who can interact in any way s/he wishes to do so.

7. After 5 minutes Number 1 will summarise what has been said by Number 2, but also how they perceived the storyteller's feelings.

8. Discuss in pairs what happened.

Feedback

Discuss in large group:

1. What it felt like to be the storyteller.

2. What it felt like to be the listener.

3. The advantages and disadvantages of the listener (i) not being able to speak, (ii) being able to interact freely.

4. Whether the reflections were accurate.

5. What did you learn for your own future practice?

TYPES OF COMMUNICATION

- Verbal

- Non-verbal

- Behavioural

- Written

THINGS TO THINK ABOUT

When communicating think about:

- Voice

- Eye contact

- Facial expressions

- Position and use of body

- Breathing

VERBAL COMMUNICATION

To improve verbal communication remember:

- Think before you speak

- Be clear about what you are saying

- Speak loud enough/not too loudly

- Do not speak too fast

- Think about the language you use

THE VOICE

Think about:

- Tone

- Pitch

- Inflection

- Spacing of words

- Use of emphases

- Pauses

- Silences

SOME USEFUL WORDS

Try to avoid using the word 'Why?' to start a question. It is better to use:

- HOW?

- WHO?

- WHAT?

- WHEN?

- WHERE?

BODY LANGUAGE

When communicating you need to be conscious of what your body is doing and showing. You need to be aware of:

- Head

- Facial expressions

- Eye contact

- Arms

- Hands

- Legs

- Feet

APPROPRIATE USE OF TOUCH

Be careful to use touch appropriately. Touch should be used to:

- Reassure

- Comfort

- Encourage

- Guide

- Stop

PRACTICAL AIDS FOR EFFECTIVE COMMUNICATION

- Hearing aids

- Loop systems

- Adaptors

- Microphone aids

- Headphones

- Doorbell/light flashes

- Alarm clocks

- Makaton/communication boards

- Electronic writing machines

- Signs

- Pictures

- Cards

- Writing paper and pen

Case Study 7.1

Celia was 70 years old when she was admitted to a home after her sister had died. Celia had been blind since birth and had always lived with members of her family in the same house. When her sister died she had no living relatives and her health had started to deteriorate. She found adapting to a new environment extremely difficult for several reasons. The home was a very large building with long corridors; she had previously lived in a small terraced house. There were 40 service users in the home; when a number of them came together either in a lounge or the dining room, Celia found it very difficult to concentrate on listening to or identifying individuals because of other noises – voices in conversation, the loudness of the television, clatter of cutlery and plates.

Discuss

1. If Celia came to live in your home or attended your day centre, what things would make it difficult for her to adapt to the environment or hinder effective communication?

2. Make a list of questions you would want to ask Celia.

3. What would you do to help Celia get to know her new surroundings?

Case Study 7.2

Daniel Armstrong has Alzheimer's disease and has been attending day centre for a month. His wife has looked after him for the past eight years but is now finding it extremely difficult to cope as she is in her 80s and has recently been diagnosed as having an under-active thyroid which is making her feel very lethargic. Daniel cannot communicate very well; he talks a lot but it is quite difficult to understand what he is saying. He can get very agitated on occasions. Since starting at day centre he keeps going over to the same corner of the room and weeing into the yukka plant. The day centre manager has spoken to Mrs Armstrong about this behaviour which he does not present at home. Today the escort comes in to tell you that she has realised that in the Armstrongs' bungalow, the bathroom is located off the lounge in exactly the same place as the yukka plant is placed from where Daniel sits at day centre.

Discuss

1. Think about how you would deal with this problem.
2. What would you say to Daniel?
3. What would you do?
4. Are there any other methods of communication which would be helpful?
5. Do you need to communicate with anyone else about this problem in the day centre or outside?

Case Study 7.3

Greta has spent most of her life in mental institutions but now lives in the community. She has been diagnosed as having schizophrenia. For the past two years she has attended your day centre during which time she has taken her medication regularly and not presented any problems. In recent weeks, Greta has started being short-tempered with day centre workers and the other service users. She has refused to participate in the activities she usually enjoys and prefers to sit quietly on her own. Staff have noticed cuts and burns on her arms; when asked about how she has sustained the injuries Greta tells staff to mind their own business. Today another service user tells you that as she came out of the toilet she saw Greta deliberately cut herself with a pair of scissors.

Discuss

1. Having read the information above, what concerns you about Greta?

2. What would you say to Greta about her self-harming behaviour?

3. Greta has made it obvious she prefers to be on her own, how are you going to communicate with her about what is going on in her life at the moment?

4. What methods of working might you adopt in the future to help Greta?

Case Study 7.4

Norman has had an emergency admission to your residential home, because he needed a place of safety. In his previous placement there have been allegations of physical abuse by members of staff. Norman, who is 65 years old, has learning disabilities and no verbal communication. He has no family or friends. When he is brought into the home by a duty social worker whom he does not know, he is crying and seems very distressed.

Discuss

1. What would you do when Norman first enters the home?
2. How are you going to communicate with Norman?
3. Could any aids help you?
4. What do you need to think about carefully?
5. The day after admission, who would you want to talk to in order to help communication with Norman?

Chapter 8

Recording

Many people hate writing. This can be for all sorts of reasons. A common experience is to have bad memories of school – spelling tests, writing essays and so on. This can taint people's views for the future. I find on a lot of training courses I provide that workers have difficulty with writing; they get nervous that they are going to be 'forced to scribe' in group work or 'shown up because I can't spell'. A good trainer would never put anyone in either of these positions. Nevertheless over the years it has made me think a lot about how to help people who do struggle with literacy problems.

There is more recognition now that people may have problems, for example, more and more people are being diagnosed with dyslexia in adulthood, which has been completely missed in childhood. Around 4 per cent of the population is severely dyslexic; a further 6 per cent have mild to moderate problems (British Dyslexia Association 2002). It is vital that workers who experience such difficulties are given adequate support. There has been such a huge increase in paperwork in recent years that record-keeping is a crucial part of most jobs in social care. Record-keeping has always been important, but probably has never been given enough emphasis or attention.

This chapter will be concerned with what is good recording. It worries me that many workers have never had any training on how to record properly. This is not a case where you can learn by doing – you need to be trained properly, but not in a way which is reminiscent of old school teaching methods.

Why have written records?

NATIONAL MINIMUM STANDARDS

37.1 Records required by regulation for the protection of service users and for the effective and efficient running of the business are maintained, up to date and accurate.

37.2 Service users have access to their records and information about them held by the home, as well as opportunities to help maintain their personal records.

37.3 Individual records and home records are secure, up to date and in good order; and are constructed, maintained and used in accordance with the Data Protection Act 1998 and other statutory requirements. (DH 2002, p.40)

Written records are a way of communicating and will help care workers in all aspects of their work. Throughout this manual the word 'accountability' keeps appearing and reference is made to the fact that every worker is accountable to a line manager and the employing organisation. Accountability can be demonstrated through written records. A written record is a way of communicating:

- what work is being undertaken (objectives)
- how work is being done (methods)
- what work has been done (monitor, review, evaluate)
- needs
- incidents/events
- opinions.

Handout 8.1, p.241

There is also the legal aspect of recording.

> Good record-keeping is an essential consideration for local authorities, so that, when they are challenged – as is increasingly likely – they are able to demonstrate that decisions were not taken unlawfully or with maladministration. (Mandelstam 1998, p.163)

This does not only apply to local authorities. Most policies and procedures of any organisation will require workers to keep a written record. There may be forms which need to be completed or the worker will be required to write in a service user's file. Each type of record will be written for a different purpose, which is the crucial starting point. Throughout this chapter key questions will be highlighted.

Written records have a number of uses which are summarised in Handout 8.2. They can act as an aid to our memory. Most of us probably have a lot on our minds – thinking about home and work – so that we suffer with 'information over-load'. So if you were asked what you were doing on this day last week would you remember? If you cannot remember then it is very unlikely that if you were asked about something that happened at work a year ago that you would be able to recall that either. If you

---

Good Practice Points

A record should explain what you did and why you did it.

When decisions are made, the reasons for making a decision should be explained.

---

have recorded something in detail, it should trigger a memory. Therefore, you should record what you did and the reason for doing it.

Recording is a real safeguard if somebody accuses a worker of doing something or of not doing something. A record should be written in a way that will help a care worker remember the sequence of events but also exactly what happened and why.

Records can be used in supervision sessions to discuss how a worker is developing. A manager will be able to see from written records how a worker is recording in files, communication books, care plans etc. Also, when a care worker has been working with a service user for a long time, it is easy to forget how things might have changed or what is now being done differently. It can be helpful for a care worker to take time out to read back over files and evaluate changes, progress or deterioration in the service user and consider how they have dealt with these things; that is, evaluate their own practice and their learning curve. Carrying this argument further, records can be used as a basis for evaluating current work and for future care planning.

Finally, it is important that care workers realise that records from a home or day centre can be used in a court of law. There could be all sorts of reasons why files may be used as evidence in Court; just two examples: a worker could be accused of committing some offence or a service user may be a victim of abuse.

Care workers in homes and day centres probably think writing is only a minor part of their job. Exercise 8.1 should make them realise just how much writing they may do.

When talking about records you might hear people refer to *running record* and *process record*, which are terms which have been in use for years. A simple explanation is that a running record is the short version and the process record is the longer, more in-depth account. A running record is useful for triggering memory and checking quickly when something happened. It is often called a 'contact sheet'.

Case Example

17.6.02 – 9.00a.m. Rang Kilner Row Surgery to ask for repeat prescription.

18.6.02 – 10.30a.m. Report arrived from Dr Carlisle, consultant physician; placed on Ethel's file.

21.6.02 – 3.22p.m. Rang Ethel's daughter, Mrs Green. Ethel wants her to bring in a new nightdress when she comes for the review next week.

24.6.02 – 1.30p.m. Helen Harris, social worker, called in to see Ethel.

24.6.02 – 2.30p.m. Social worker asked me to ring chiropodist, Susan Wood, for Ethel. Made appointment for 1.7.02 @ 11.00a.m.

28.6.02 – 2.00 to 3.00p.m. Review – see notes on file.

A process record will record events in much more detail. Not everything that happens in a service user's life will need to be recorded in depth. Some examples where in-depth recording might be necessary are:

- when a service user discloses important information

- when an incident occurs

- keyworker session.

Handout 8.3 illustrates the different types of written communication a care worker might be involved in. Thought should also be given to *where* information is written; for example:

- files
- communication books
- diaries
- telephone message pads (preferably with carbon sheets)
- forms/charts.

Who we write records for

Mention has already been made of the fact that records can be used in all sorts of ways, which means that different people can read them:

- service user
- staff within the organisation
- manager
- colleagues
- professionals
- other agencies.

There will obviously be restrictions on access because of confidentiality and access issues, which will be discussed below. When a care worker sits down to write any record, s/he should ask the basic question: 'Who are you writing the record for?'

Key Question

Who are you writing the record for?

Confidentiality and access to records

The Data Protection Act 1998, which was introduced in March 2000, is concerned with personal information and data which is stored in files or records on a computer. It is not the purpose of this manual to go into detail about the Data Protection Act, but care workers should be aware of the basic principles:

1.   Personal data shall be processed fairly and lawfully.

2. Personal data shall be obtained only for one or more specified and lawful purposes, and shall not be further processed in any manner incompatible with the purpose or those purposes.

3. Personal data shall be adequate, relevant and not excessive in relation to the purpose or purposes for which they are processed.

4. Personal data shall be accurate and, where necessary, kept up to date.

5. Personal data processed for any purpose or purposes shall not be kept for longer than is necessary for that purpose or purposes for which it was obtained.

6. Personal data shall be processed in accordance with the rights of data subjects under this Act.

7. Appropriate technical and organisational measures shall be taken against unauthorised or unlawful processing of personal data and against accidental loss or destruction of, or damage to, personal data.

8. Personal data shall not be transferred to a country or territory outside the European Economic Area (i.e. E.U. Member states plus Iceland, Lichtenstein and Norway) unless that country or territory ensures an adequate level of protection for the rights and freedoms of data subjects in relation to the processing of personal data.

A service user has the right to see any information which is held about them in a home or day centre; that information must be kept confidential and secure.

Care workers should also be aware that there are 6 Caldicott Principles that govern the use of patient-identifiable (service user) information, which are consistent with the Data Protection Act 1998. These are:

1. Justify the purpose.

2. Don't use patient-identifiable information unless it is absolutely necessary.

3. Use the minimum necessary patient-identifiable information.

4. Access to patient-identifiable information should be on a strict need-to-know basis.

5. Everyone with access to patient-identifiable information should be aware of his or her responsibilities.

6. Understand and comply with the law.

(Caldicott Committee 1997)

The Department of Health has stated the principles of confidentiality as:

- Information should be used only for the purposes for which it was given.

- Information about a user/patient should normally be shared only with the consent of that person.

- Information should be shared on a 'need to know' basis.

- Users and carers should be advised why and with whom information concerning them has been shared.

- All confidential information should be rigorously safeguarded. (Department of Health 1991)

Any decision to share information without the consent of the source and subject should be based on a careful balancing of:

1. the rights of the source and/or subject to confidentiality at common law, and privacy under Article 8 of the European Convention on Human Rights (ECHR). These rights should be taken to include rights to reputation and livelihood, and the privacy of both one's home and correspondence; and

2. the harm likely to result from not sharing the information.

Practitioners should also bear in mind the human rights of all adults, including those who are vulnerable, to be protected from treatment which is 'inhuman or degrading' (Article 3, ECHR).

Exercise 8.2 should help care workers to think about issues surrounding confidentiality and the sharing of information.

Content

Everyone has picked up a file or report at one time or another and thought that what was written was either good or bad. But what exactly made it good or bad? This is what care workers need to focus on. They need to think about what they expect from others and what people might expect from them in a written record. Exercise 8.3 is designed to focus care workers on this. Every record will have a different purpose, so content may need to differ.

I am often told by workers that people have told them they write too much. One cannot prescribe length; relevance is the key. This goes back to questioning why the record is being written in the first place and for whom.

Writing the facts is important, but a care worker must be clear about how these facts have been obtained. Is the fact known because the care worker was there at the time (i.e. direct observation) or has somebody given the information?

Key Questions

Do I know this has definitely happened?

How do I know?

Who saw this happen?

Somebody like a GP may give their professional opinion, whereas a service user who talks about what think they heard through the wall is only giving hearsay information. If someone does express an opinion exactly who that person is must be written in the record and it must be made clear in what capacity they are giving that opinion. It is also important to state where an opinion is given and that it may not be a fact.

Key Questions

Whose opinion is this?

Is the person qualified to assess/give an opinion?

Recording needs to be systematic and in detail. It is important to record who did what and when.

Key Question

WHO did **WHAT** and **WHEN?**

To summarise, good content needs to be:

- relevant

- objective

- factual

- clear

- concise

- accurate

- non-judgemental

- non-discriminatory.

Handout 8.4, p.244

Layout

How a written record looks will affect the reader; if one sees hard to read or untidy handwriting it is immediately off-putting. Good layout is an important part of recording. A care worker needs to think about how they will present written information and in order to do this some planning needs to take place. In training or a supervision session, it is helpful to go through the different ways in which a record can be set out. This should be done in an interesting way, not in a school-like fashion, which may bring back bad memories for some people. Exercise 8.4 is one way of facilitating this. It is important that a care worker realises that different things can be used to make the presentation attractive to the reader, namely:

- legible handwriting

- black pen

- paragraphs

- headings/sub-headings

- numbering/lettering, e.g. 1, 2, 3; (i), (ii), (iii); a), b), c)

- bullet points

- asterisks

- capitals

- bold

- italics

- underline

- quotations

- punctuation.

Handout 8.5, p.245

Preparation

Care workers are always under pressure and will have time constraints; this is no excuse to avoid recording. The importance of recording has to be emphasised to a care worker and the fact that it has to be made a priority. In order to write good records a care worker needs to sit down and plan; that is, preparation is imperative. A useful reminder when thinking about writing is that one communicates in writing to:

- describe

- explain

- inform

- argue for.

Therefore, a care worker must:

- sit and think

- plan

- draft

- write (and maybe rewrite).

Handout 8.6, p.246

When planning to write a starting point is to ask the following question:

Key Question

WHY is this being written
and **WHO** is it being written for?

It is important to give structure to a written record; thinking in simple ways can be useful – for example:

- beginning

- middle

- end.

Good Practice Point

Remember to put: Date, time, signature.

Handout 8.7 is an example of how this simple structure could be used in a process record.

When preparing for a review or when there are concerns about a service user it is useful to plan a written report by thinking around the following headings:

- aims/objectives

- achievements/failures

- problems/difficulties

- developments

- reassessment of risk

- other assessments needed

- review

- summary.

Handout 8.8, p.248

Whenever writing about a service user it is vital to include the service user's views. Workers in many different jobs often fail to think about asking a service user to contribute to their own file – rarely are files shown or shared with a service user on a regular basis. A care worker should remember that such involvement is promoting working in partnership with the service user. It is imperative that a service user's views, opinions and feelings are recorded.

Case Example

Gillian had always enjoyed writing poetry. When she came to live in the home, she continued to write poetry about all sorts of things, including what happened to her in the home and how she felt about these things. She shared these poems with her keyworker, who suggested that some of them could be kept in her file. The poems were read out by Gillian at her annual review.

Messages

When workers are dashing around it is easy to scribble messages on bits of paper which may be to hand. This is not good enough. Messages must be written in a correct way either on a message pad (preferably with carbon sheets) or in a communications book. If a message is received by telephone or given in person the following information should be written down:

- date and time of call/visit
- name of caller/visitor and their position
- telephone contact number/or address
- the message
- print name of person who took the message and job title
- signature of person taking message.

Handout 8.9, p.249

Handout 8.10 summarises some basic dos and don'ts for good written records.

Exercises to practise recording

Exercises 8.5, 8.6 and 8.7 can be used to help care workers improve their recording skills.

Helping workers

If workers do struggle with writing, there are many useful books which explain grammar and punctuation simply. Some of these are detailed below.

Suggested reading

British Dyslexia Association (April 2002) *What is Dyslexia?* AO1. Reading: British Dyslexia Association.

Hilton, C. and Hyder, M. (1998) *Getting to Grips with Punctuation and Grammar.* London: Letts Educational.

Hopkins, G. (1998a) *Plain English for Social Services: A Guide to Better Communication.* Lyme Regis: Russell House Publishing.

Hopkins, G. (1998b) *The Write Stuff: A Guide to Effective Writing in Social Care and Related Services.* Lyme Regis: Russell House Publishing.

Useful organisation

British Dyslexia Association

98 London Road, Reading RG1 5AU

Tel: 0118 966 2677 Fax: 0118 935 1927 Helpline: 0118 966 8271

E-mail (Helpline): info@dyslexiahelp-bda.demon.co.uk

(Admin): admin@bda-dyslexia.demon.co.uk Website: www.bda-dyslexia.org.uk

VIDEOS

Effective Communication 2

Role of the Care Worker

WHAT DO YOU WRITE?

Objective

To prove to care workers that written work does form an important part of their job and to illustrate just how often they probably do write on the job.

Participants

Individual.

Equipment

Paper and pen.
Copy of Handout 8.3 if required.

Time

10 minutes.

Task

1. Think about when you have been on shift over the past week. Try to remember every situation you were in when you had to write something down.

2. Make a list of the types of things you wrote and where you wrote them.

Feedback

To manager or colleague.

Note for trainer

Handout 8.3 can be given out after the exercise has been completed. The list is not exhaustive.

DEFINING CONFIDENTIALITY

Objective

To make care workers think about what confidentiality means to them in their work role.

Participants

To work individually and then in a large group.

Equipment

Trainer to give each participant half a sheet of A4 paper.

Time

5 minutes to write definition; 20 minutes group discussion.

Task

1. Think about what confidentiality means to you in your work role.

2. Write a definition of confidentiality – 'Confidentiality is…' – on the piece of paper which has been given to you.

3. Fold the piece of paper in half and half again. Throw it into the middle of the floor.

4. Trainer collects pieces of paper, shuffles them and gives one piece of paper to each participant.

5. In turn each participant reads out the definition on the piece of paper they have been given and then pauses. Participants are asked to comment on the definition which has been read out.

6. Open discussion.

Note for trainer

It is important to make this exercise very safe. When explaining the exercise to participants you must tell them:

1. A **ground rule** is that the author of the definition will not be identified so that people will speak freely.

2. If someone gets their own definition back or they recognise someone's handwriting, they should not say so.

3. Participants can ask for the definition to be read out again.

WHAT MAKES GOOD CONTENT?

Objective

To make care workers think about what makes a good written record.

Participants

Large group exercise.

Equipment

Trainer to use flipchart stand, paper and pens.
Copies of Handout 8.4.

Time

15 minutes.

Task

1. Trainer asks the large group to think about what makes good content.

2. Trainer lists comments on flipchart paper.

3. Trainer facilitates open discussion.

4. Trainer pins sheets on wall after exercise is complete.

5. Trainer gives out Handout 8.4 and discusses.

WHAT MAKES GOOD LAYOUT?

Objective

To make care workers think how to present a written record.

Participants

Large group exercise.

Equipment

Trainer to use flipchart stand, paper and pens.
Copies of Handout 8.5.

Time

15 minutes.

Task

1.   Trainer asks the large group to think about what makes a written record look good.

2.   Trainer lists comments on flipchart paper.

3.   Trainer facilitates open discussion.

4.   Trainer pins sheets on wall after exercise is complete.

5.   Trainer gives out Handout 8.5.

WHAT DID YOU DO THIS MORNING?

Objective

To illustrate how good a care worker's recall is and to review how records are written.

Participants

Individual.

Equipment

Paper and pens.

Time

15–20 minutes.

Task

1. Think back to when you got up this morning. Take yourself through everything you have done since then.

2. Write a true written record of what you have done this morning. Set it out as though you were recording it on a service user file – you being the service user.

Feedback

Share your record with someone (e.g. manager or colleague) and ask them to comment on the record.

RECORDING WHAT YOU SEE

Objective

To practise observational skills and recording skills.

Participants

Stage 1 will be undertaken individually; participants will then work in pairs and larger groups.

Equipment

Trainer to provide a video which shows several short scenes in quick succession, e.g. the beginning of **Abuse in the Care Home**. Paper and pens.

Time

30 minutes.

Task

1. Trainer shows part of a video.

2. Participants are asked to write a true written record of what they have just watched.

3. Participants go into pairs and give their partner the written record to read. They then discuss what was good or bad about the record and, crucially, whether it was accurate.

Feedback

Group discussion to focus on accuracy, content, layout etc.

RECORDING WHAT YOU HEAR

Objective

To practise listening, observational and recording skills.

Participants

Stage 1 will be undertaken individually; participants will then work in pairs and larger groups.

Equipment

Paper and pens.

Time

30 minutes.

Task

1. A dialogue will take place for 5 minutes between two participants in front of the rest of the group. The trainer will give the pair a subject to talk about.

2. Participants are asked to write a true written record of what they have just watched.

3. Participants go into pairs and give their partner the written record to read. They then discuss what was good or bad about the record.

Feedback

Group discussion to focus on accuracy, content, layout etc.

WRITTEN RECORDS CAN COMMUNICATE

- What work is being undertaken (objectives)

- How work is being done (methods)

- What work has been done (monitor, review, evaluate)

- Needs

- Incidents/events

- Opinions

WHY WE NEED TO RECORD

- Accountability

- To explain and justify actions

- To give reasons for decisions made

- Acts as an aid to memory

- Safeguard against allegations

- Tool for monitoring, reviewing and evaluating work with the service user

- Tool for the worker to learn and be objective

- Basis for risk assessment and care planning

- Records may be needed in a court of law

WHAT A CARE WORKER MIGHT WRITE

- Notes (for service users' files, in meetings, to colleagues, on training courses)

- Letters

- Memos

- Reports for meetings (e.g. for review or case conference)

- Forms

- Contracts/agreements

- Activity sheets

- Shopping lists

- Receipts

- Messages

- Risk assessments

- Care plans

- Supervision notes

- Medication notes

- Rotas

- Menus

- Notices

GOOD CONTENT

- Relevant

- Objective

- Factual

- Clear

- Concise

- Accurate

- Non-judgemental

- Non-discriminatory

GOOD LAYOUT

Use a variety of things to make a document look user friendly:

- Legible handwriting

- Black pen

- Paragraphs

- Headings/sub-headings

- Numbering/lettering, e.g. 1, 2, 3; (i), (ii), (iii); a), b), c)

- Bullet points

- Asterisks

- Capitals

- Bold

- Italics

- Underline

- Quotations

- Punctuation

PREPARATION

You communicate in writing to:

- Describe

- Explain

- Inform

- Argue for

Therefore, a care worker must:

- Sit and think

- Plan

- Draft

- Write (and maybe rewrite)

STRUCTURING A PROCESS RECORD

Beginning

- Name of service user and date of birth

- Date and time (of meeting, incident)

- Who was present (name of person and their job, role)

- Purpose of meeting/contact

Middle

- What you want to record

- Facts

- Opinions

- Service user's wishes/feelings

End

- Summary of key points

- Conclusions

- Action agreed with service user

- Name and job title of person writing the record

- Signature

- Date and time record written

- Location

WRITING FOR REVIEWING PURPOSES

- Aims/objectives

- Achievements/failures

- Problems/difficulties

- Developments

- Reassessment of risk

- Other assessments needed

- Review

- Summary

TAKING MESSAGES

- Date and time of call/visit

- Name of caller/visitor and their position

- Telephone contact number/or address

- The message

- Print name of person who took the message and job title

- Signature of person taking message

DOS AND DON'TS FOR WRITTEN RECORDS

DO

- Use black pen

- Cross out mistakes with just one black line and initial

- Check what you have written

- Record regularly

- Record as soon as possible after the event

DON'T

- Use Tippex

- Write long sentences

- Be vague

- Waffle

- Use jargon

- Use cliches

- Use shorthand

- Use abbreviations

Chapter 9

Supervision

Giving supervision to workers was one of my favourite tasks when I was a manager. This was probably due to the fact that I had always had a very positive experience of supervision myself when I was a practising social worker. I felt I had learnt so much from the managers who had given me supervision over the years that I always vowed that I would try to develop any workers I supervised in the same way. Now that I provide training courses on supervision, I endeavour to impart enthusiasm for the subject area. Unfortunately, not everyone shares my viewpoint. I am often met with resistance when course participants tell me: 'We haven't got time to do supervision. We've got to get on with the job.' The starting point for this chapter is to explain why supervision is a vital part of the job of being a care worker. Supervision is about learning and development.

Why supervision is important

The overall objective of supervising workers is to ensure that a good quality service is being provided to service users. The four functions of supervision will be discussed in detail below. This should help a care worker to have a better understanding of how supervision should be a positive and beneficial experience if it is done well. In simple terms supervision should be in place to help and support the care worker. It should be a forum where a care worker can talk about:

- how the job is going
- any difficulties which are being experienced
- ways of working
- feelings
- development and training needs.

Handout 9.1, p.272

Through supervision a manager should get to know each care worker and learn about how they are functioning in their role of providing care to service users. Formal supervision should be used in conjunction with observing the care worker.

Supervision policies

Most organisations should have a supervision policy in place. A new care worker needs to check this out if their manager has not shown them or made reference to the policy during induction. A supervision policy should include guidance about:

- the importance of supervision and the organisation's commitment to it
- the definition of supervision
- aims and objectives
- the roles and responsibilities of supervisors and supervisees
- promoting anti-discriminatory practice
- minimum expected frequency
- standards
- the contract
- supervision notes
- the boundaries of confidentiality/sharing information.

Handout 9.2, p.273

Experience of supervision

I have already said that my own experience of being supervised was always good, but sadly not everyone has the same experience and this can affect how a worker may view the importance of supervision. If a worker has never had a good experience of supervision, then it is very unlikely that s/he is going to see the point of 'wasting time in supervision, when I could be getting on with the job'.

Managers have a responsibility to provide useful supervision which will develop their staff. Organisations need to ensure that they offer training to managers so that they know what they should be doing; that is, any supervisor must have a theoretical base from which to start. A supervisor cannot 'just do it'. It is also important that care workers have formal training on the purpose of supervision.

Blocks

We all have 'hang-ups' about certain things; sometimes these can stop you facing things or getting on – that is, they block you. Your past experiences of supervision may block you from gaining a positive experience in the future. Exercise 9.1 will help care workers discuss their experiences of supervision. So what else might stop you getting something from your current supervision sessions? The following are some of the thoughts which have been disclosed to me:

253

- 'I'm scared she'll [manager] think I'm useless.'

- 'I don't like talking.'

- 'I find it difficult to explain myself. I just do the job.'

- 'It's just a way of checking up on us.'

- 'I don't trust him [manager]. He gossips with other staff.'

Functions of supervision

NATIONAL MINIMUM STANDARDS

36.3   Supervision covers:

- all aspects of practice

- philosophy of care in the home

- career development needs. (DH 2002, p.40)

A great number of texts exist on supervision and a care worker would not be expected to plough their way through all of them in order to understand the theories relating to supervision. However, it is useful to look back and see how the theory has developed, and to refer to some of the standard texts when considering the functions of supervision.

For a very long time traditional texts talked about the three basic functions of supervision which Kadushin (1976) described as educative, supportive and managerial. In the 1990s Richards and Payne introduced a fourth function which is now widely accepted. They summarise the four functions as:

- *The management function*: ensuring that agency policies and practices are understood and adhered to; prioritising and allocating the work; managing the workload; setting the objectives and evaluating the effectiveness of what is done.

- *The educational function*: helping staff to continue to learn and to develop professionally, so that they are able both to cope with societal and organisational demands and to initiate fresh ways of approaching the work, according to changing needs.

- *The supportive function*: enabling staff to cope with the many stresses that the work entails.

- *The mediation function*: to represent staff needs to higher management, to negotiate what services need to be co-ordinated, to clarify to others outside the agency the legal and resource constraints or requirements within which the team is operating.

(Richards and Payne 1990, pp.13–14)

Handout 9.3, p.274

Management function

Everyone who works for an organisation is accountable to someone. A care worker is accountable to their manager, who in turn will be accountable to someone higher up the ladder. A worker must explain what they are doing in the job and it is the manager's role to check that they are functioning in an appropriate way. The manager's role is to ensure that policies and procedures are being implemented and that good practice is being promoted. To use the new 'buzz' words, it is about standards, competence and performance.

> ## Case Example
>
> Manager to new care worker: 'I know when we last had supervision you were feeling a bit overwhelmed with all the policies and procedures that I showed you in the manual. Today I'd like to talk about that and see how you're getting on, but I also want to talk particularly about recording. I have been looking at some of your notes in the communications book and the care plans you have started to write.'

Education function

None of us can ever know everything. Even if we have been doing our job a long time and we think we are good at it, there is always something else to learn. Supervision should be a useful forum where a care worker can highlight their needs for further education and training. It is important that a care worker is made to feel comfortable enough in supervision to admit that they do not know something or are finding an aspect of the work difficult. A supervisor will work on identifying strengths and weaknesses in skills, knowledge and understanding and as a result will be able to identify training needs.

A point which was made in the previous chapter was that some care workers may struggle with literacy issues. A supervision session should be the place where a care worker can talk in confidence about their difficulties and where the supervisor can offer help and support.

As well as identifying training needs, the supervisor should be able to share knowledge so that the care worker can learn during the supervision session. Different methods of helping a care worker to learn will be discussed below.

Case Example

Anne-Marie was the keyworker for Edgar who had just been told he was terminally ill. Anne-Marie told her manager in supervision that she wanted to support Edgar as best she could, but she knew very little about death and dying. The manager contacted the training section in the department to find out if there were any courses which could help Anne-Marie; she also rang the local Cruse office and asked them to send some leaflets.

Support

Support which is offered in supervision should be both practical and emotional. During a supervision session a care worker should be able to talk openly about their practice and the supervisor should be offering practical advice through discussion and other learning methods. Emotional support is also crucial, because everyone needs to talk about how they feel. Being a care worker is not an easy job; it is hard physically and emotionally. Care staff have to deal with many stressful or disturbing situations. It is important that a care worker is given the opportunity to vent their feelings and not fear that they will be seen as 'not coping'. It is important that feelings are dealt with in the work situation and that care workers do not offload in their family/home situation, as they may be breaking confidentiality.

Case Example

Jason is 20 years old and works in a day centre. He is very angry when he comes into supervision today. When the manager asks him what is wrong he explains that he is feeling both angry and upset because one of the service users, Fanny, has come to the centre covered in cuts and bruises. She has openly disclosed that her husband physically abuses her, but she does not want to do anything about it. The manager suggests that Jason talks about his feelings first of all and then they will discuss the Vulnerable Adult Abuse Policy and Procedure.

Mediation

A care worker may feel that they are a little cog in a big wheel and that they cannot change anything. This is not true. It is important that a care worker voices their views on what is good and bad within an organisation or what is lacking – for example, the needs of staff, resources, not meeting service users' needs and so on. It is the responsibility of a manager to take these views higher (to senior managers or owners of a home) or to other appropriate agencies. In this way, staff within a home or day centre can influence allocation of resources and policy formation, and advocate on behalf of service users. It also works the other way – a manager has to bring issues and information back down from owners/management to staff.

Case Example

There used to be two buses which brought service users to Cromwell Day Centre. With cut-backs there is now only one, which has to do two runs. As a result of this, some service users are getting to the centre much later than they used to do, which they are angry about. Staff do not think it is fair either as the day is now very short for some of the service users and some of them have to spend a longer time on the bus. Each day centre worker has raised this in supervision and the manager has now agreed to take it higher.

Starting supervision

When a supervisor and supervisee meet for the first time, they need to discuss what they expect from the sessions and from each other. A new care worker may never have experienced supervision; therefore, a manager should take time to explain its purpose and what will happen. For more experienced workers, it is important to reflect back on what supervision has been like in the past. To do this Exercise 9.1 can be utilised in a training session or when a new supervisor is going to take over. All adults learn differently; a manager needs to find out how a care worker will learn and implement the appropriate methods (Honey and Mumford 2000a and 2000b). Again, reflecting back on past experiences can help to plan for the future. Exercises 9.2 and 9.3 can be used to focus such discussions.

Making a contract

Exercise 9.2 aims to get a care worker to think about what they expect from supervision. The work produced during this exercise can be used to formulate a supervision contract. As stated earlier, an organisation's supervision policy may have a standard supervision contract in place. Nevertheless, before commencing supervision sessions, a supervisor and supervisee should meet together to discuss their expectations and to formulate a written contract. If supervision has been taking place without a written contract being in place, then a supervision session should be organised to discuss this and formulate a contract which should cover the following areas:

- frequency
- time
- duration
- location
- format
- setting the agenda
- regular items for discussion
- preparation for supervision sessions
- recording of supervision sessions
- boundaries of confidentiality
- storage of notes
- appraisals
- review of contract.

Handout 9.4, p.275

Frequency

An organisation's policy should state the minimum requirement regarding supervision sessions.

NATIONAL MINIMUM STANDARDS

36.1   Care staff receive formal supervision at least 6 times a year. (DH 2002, p.39)

Time

In some work settings it is possible to set a regular time for supervision sessions. However, this is less likely to happen in homes and day centres because of staff working rota systems. This can cause problems too in that staff may swap shifts with colleagues and then have to rearrange a booked supervision. It is important that staff see supervision as a priority and not something that 'can be put off'.

Duration

The supervisor and supervisee must discuss how long they think supervision sessions might last. Neither person should be putting appointments in their diary so that they are rushing to get to or leave a session. Supervision should be carried out in a relaxed atmosphere where the people involved are not worried about time pressures.

Location

A supervision session should be located in a place which is free from interruption and where no one can overhear what is being said.

Case Example

Janet had worked in a number of care homes before taking up her new position in Ivory House. When she went for her first supervision session the manager said they would meet in her office. After half an hour Janet politely told the manager that she did not feel comfortable having supervision in the office for several reasons:

- The manager was sitting behind her desk. It made Janet feel as though there was a barrier between them.

- Staff kept coming in to get things out of the filing cabinet (even though there was a 'Do Not Disturb' sign on the door).

- The telephone kept ringing.

Format

As stated above, everyone learns in different ways. Below there will be a discussion about the different methods of supervision. Methods to be adopted should be discussed and written into the contract.

Setting the agenda

There should be an agenda for a supervision session. Agreement should be reached as to when the supervisor and supervisee can inform each other about items which need to be put on the agenda; that is, how much notice needs to be given so they can prepare.

Regular items for discussion

There may be subject items/topics which need to be discussed at every supervision session. These should be written clearly into the contract.

Case Example

Six months ago Marion disclosed to her manager that she felt she was 'sinking'. She felt she had 'taken too much on all at once'. She had started her NVQ in Care Level 3 a year ago, which she was enjoying but was finding hard. At the same time she had become a registered foster parent and had had two placements. More recently her mother had been ill and was staying temporarily with Marion and her family. Marion loved her job but felt she had to reduce her working hours. She valued her supervision sessions and her contract had the following items written in for discussion at each session:

1. time management

2. NVQ

3. home situation.

Preparation for supervision sessions

A care worker should not go into a supervision session without having given some thought to it. As stated above, items need to be put on an agenda, so people involved in supervision can prepare beforehand. A supervisor might also expect the care worker to have done some work or a task for the session. These expectations should be included in the contract.

Recording of supervision sessions

Notes must be taken during a supervision session. Usually it is expected that the supervisor will take the notes but there is nothing to stop an agreement being made that the care worker will take responsibility for note-taking if there is a valid reason for this. When the notes have been written they should be shared with the parties involved. If there are any inaccuracies or omissions these should be rectified, after which both parties sign the notes, which are then photocopied. All parties involved should have their own copy.

Confidentiality

Once again a supervision policy should make a statement about the boundaries of confidentiality and what the organisation expects from its staff. A supervisor must make it clear when information may be taken elsewhere; that is, to a senior manager, personnel department etc. Some workers may choose to talk about personal matters in supervision which they may not want other people to be privy to; agreement needs to be reached about what is recorded and shared.

If supervision notes are to be typed up, the supervisee needs to be made aware of who might undertake this task. Personal information may be given in a supervision session which the supervisee might not want shared with other staff.

Case Example

Clare, who was a day centre worker, told her manager in supervision that she was pregnant again. She had already had three miscarriages. She asked the manager not to tell anyone she was pregnant at this early stage. The manager did not write this information in the supervision notes because they were normally typed up by the administrative assistant who worked in the residential home where the day centre was located.

Storage of notes

Supervision notes should be locked away in a safe place. A care worker needs to know that no one else will have access to the notes.

Appraisals

Organisations may have a policy regarding the frequency of appraisals and this will be linked to the process of supervision. Appraisals are useful to reflect back on a specific period of time and consider a worker's developments, successes, failures, weaknesses and strengths and to set objectives for the future.

Review of contract

A supervision contract needs to be reviewed regularly. A date should be written in for review.

Format of supervision

Many people visualise supervision as sitting down with someone and talking. This does happen, but the reality is that supervision can happen in a variety of ways. It can be planned or happen on an ad hoc basis (i.e. when and where needed); it may be formal or informal. Payne and Scott (1985) describe supervision in the following ways:

1. Supervision takes the form of planned meetings on an individual or group basis; with an agreed agenda and methods for reaching objectives. Such meetings can be arranged for a limited or indefinite period of time, for general or specific purposes.

2. Supervision takes the form of unplanned discussions and consultations on an individual or group basis, where the agenda has to be agreed on the spot; often when an unforeseen crisis or problem has arisen. However, some space and time is created away from service-delivery to work on the problem.

3. Agreements are reached between individuals and members of a group to give help, advice, constructive criticism and other forms of feedback, while working with clients or carrying out other service delivery tasks. These agreements are made in advance, according to predetermined objectives, and made subject to monitoring and regular review.

4. Supervision is tacitly given while individuals are working with clients or engaged in service delivery tasks. It may take the form of help, advice, constructive criticism or offered through demonstration and example. This activity may become the focus for discussion in a more formal context or be developed into an explicit supervision agreement; but first occurs as unplanned activity because of needs and circumstances.

(Payne and Scott 1985, Part 1, p.29)

Supervision can take place in many different ways; it does not have to be on a one-to-one basis. As a common problem is lack of time for many staff groups in homes and day centres, a manager might want to think about adopting different approaches to supervision.

- **One to one**: manager or senior member of staff supervises one member of staff.

- **Paired**: manager or senior member of staff supervises two members of staff together.

- **Peer**: workers with the same level of responsibility supervise each other.

- **Group**: workers on the same level are supervised together in small groups with a senior person supervising.

- **Team**: the whole staff group in a workplace are supervised together.

Handout 9.5, p.276

Methods of supervision

A care worker should look forward to supervision, not dread it. It *must* be beneficial to the worker and it is the responsibility of the supervisor to find out how this can happen. A supervisor will have developed their own supervisory style and it is not the purpose of this manual to go into detail about this, but it will affect how the supervisor might conduct sessions and what methods will be used. The main styles may be:

1. task centred
2. person centred
3. interaction centred.

As suggested earlier, a manager should be trained how to supervise and during this training should be given the opportunity to consider their own supervisory style and methods. Heron's six categories of helping interventions is a useful tool for analysis, both for the supervisor and the supervisee:

- Interventions can be **authoritative/directive**, i.e. the supervisor uses authority to be:

  1. **Prescriptive**: gives advice, instruction
  2. **Informative**: gives information
  3. **Confrontative**: gives feedback, challenges

- or **facilitative**, i.e. the supervisor values what the supervisee brings:

  4. **Cathartic**: encourages expression of feelings
  5. **Catalytic**: encourages reflection and problem-solving
  6. **Supportive**: confirms, validates the individual.

(Heron 1975)

Handout 9.6, p.277

What a care worker needs to be aware of is that every human being will learn differently. The subject of adult learning is a huge one and both supervisors and supervisees should receive some training on this and on how to ascertain how a worker may learn best. There are many interesting exercises which can be undertaken to find out your learning styles – some of the best ones having been developed by Honey and Mumford (2000a and 2000b).

Another useful theory to explore is Kolb's learning cycle, which includes experience, reflection, conceptualisation and active experimentation:

- *Experience*

  We gain experience in all sorts of ways – actually seeing things, e.g. learning on the job; or seeking to learn by reading, obtaining information from other people or sources.

- *Reflection*

  The reflective worker looks back on what they have experienced and tries to make sense of the experience.

- *Conceptualisation*

  The worker analyses the experiences, raises questions and forms hypotheses (ideas about ways of working).

- *Active experimentation*

  The worker tries out ways of working.

(Kolb 1984)

Supervision should not just be about talking. The supervisor should introduce other methods in order to make the sessions interesting; for example:

- rehearsal/role play/simulation

- demonstration

- modelling

- shadowing

- set tasks

- exercises.

Handout 9.7, p.278

If a care worker fears supervision it is important for the supervisor to keep emphasising the purpose of supervision; that is, to encourage personal and professional development. A worker should never be forced to do activities which they find difficult, but it is possible to experiment with different methods in a safe environment. Role play is disliked by many people, but it is a very useful way of anticipating situations and practising.

Obviously there will be discussion in a supervision session and this can take place in a variety of ways:

- Discussion about workload, service users, practice, policies/procedures, training courses, reviewing, particular subjects.

- Supervising from case files/written records.

- Planning future work: setting objectives, trying out new ways of working.

- Using problem solving techniques.

- Suggesting books/articles to read for later discussion.

- Exercises/tasks for next session which involve written work which can then be discussed. Exercises within this training manual could be used or there are certain exercises/techniques which are useful in group supervision. For example, focusing on a problem and getting group responses; keeping a diary – the worker keeps a diary of what s/he has done, and her/his thoughts and feelings, between supervision sessions and this forms a basis for discussion.

Team development days

Lack of time and work pressures are always a problem, but also excuses for not putting aside time to promote team development. Staff meetings tend to be dominated by pressing work issues and giving/sharing information. Therefore, for a team to develop properly it is necessary to commit time specifically to focus on development work. Ideally, staff should meet away from the workplace so that this can happen without interruption, but it does mean having to arrange cover for staff.

Exercises

A manager may be expected to train staff formally and should be offered the opportunity to go on a 'Training the Trainers' course. Many training techniques can be adapted for use in a supervision session, whatever form it is taking. Questions or tasks can be set so that they can be worked on in the session or for the supervisee to do between the sessions. Below are some questions which can be set; they can be worked on by an individual worker privately or in a group work situation.

- What motivates you?

- What are your main sources of stress at home/work?

- What support systems do you have in place?

- Share a botch up (a supervisee is asked to share something they have not done very well).

- What do you worry about, fear, dread at work?

- What would you say if... [insert scenarios]?

- What would you do if... [insert scenarios]?

Some useful general topics for discussion in order to promote good practice are:

- oppressive practice

- stress and relaxation

- assertiveness

- time management

- workload management

- setting goals

- prioritising

- developing strategies

- recording

- where/how to obtain information.

Suggested reading

Hawkins, P. and Shohet, R. (2000) *Supervision in the Helping Professions.* Buckingham: Open University Press.

Heron, J. (1975) *Six Category Intervention Analysis.* Guildford: University of Surrey.

Honey, P. and Mumford, A. (2000a) *The Learning Styles Helper's Guide.* Maidenhead: Peter Honey Publications.

Honey, P. and Mumford, A. (2000b) *The Learning Styles Questionnaire (80-item version).* Maidenhead: Peter Honey Publications.

Morrison, T. (2001) *Staff Supervision in Social Care.* Brighton: Pavilion Publishing.

Pritchard, J. (ed) (1995) *Good Practice in Supervision.* London: Jessica Kingsley Publishers.

Useful organisation

Peter Honey Learning Publications Limited

10 Linden Avenue, Maidenhead, Berkshire SL6 6HB

Tel: 01628 633946 Fax: 01628 633 262

E-mail: info@peterhoney.com

Website: www.peterhoneylearning.com

📼 VIDEOS

Supervision

Role of the Care Worker

EXPERIENCES OF SUPERVISION

Objective

For care workers to evaluate their own experiences of supervision.

Participants

To be done by a care worker on their own; then shared with the line manager or another care worker.

Equipment

Paper and pen.

Time

10 minutes.

Task

1. Think about when you have had supervision and who has supervised you in the past and now in your current post.

2. Draw a line down the middle of the sheet of paper, so you have two columns. Put a heading **Good** at the top of one column and **Bad** at the top of the other.

3. Write down what was good and bad about your experiences of supervision.

Feedback

To manager or another care worker.

SHOPPING LIST: EXPECTATIONS OF SUPERVISION

Objective

For care workers to be clear about what they expect from supervision sessions and their supervisor.

Participants

To be done by a care worker on their own; then to be shared with supervisor.

Equipment

Paper and pen.

Time

15 minutes.

Task

1. Think about what you should get out of a supervision session (e.g. what should happen in it, what you should talk about etc.).

2. Make a list of your expectations.

3. Think about what is missing from your supervision sessions now.

4. Make a list of what is not being provided in your current supervision, which you think you need.

Feedback

To supervisor.

WHO AND WHAT INFLUENCES YOU?

Objective

For a care worker to think about who has influenced them in the past with a view to helping them to ask their supervisor to help in a similar way.

Participants

To be done by a care worker on their own.

Equipment

Paper and pen.

Time

15 minutes.

Task

1. Think about the people who have had an effect on you in your life; that is, people you have taken notice of and who have directly affected/influenced how you have developed as a person. Think of people in your personal life as well as your working life.

2. List the people you have thought about, separating them into 'personal' and 'work'.

3. Now think about each person you have listed. What was it about them that made you take notice of them? Why could they influence you?

4. Make a list of the 'qualities' these influential people possessed.

Feedback

To supervisor or another care worker.

SUPERVISION FOR THE CARE WORKER

Supervision should be a forum where a care worker can talk about:

- How the job is going

- Any difficulties which are being experienced

- Ways of working

- Feelings

- Development and training needs

SUPERVISION POLICY

Organisations should have a supervision policy in place which includes information and guidance on:

- The importance of supervision and the organisation's commitment to it

- The definition of supervision

- Aims and objectives

- The roles and responsibilities of supervisors and supervisees

- Promoting anti-discriminatory practice

- Minimum expected frequency

- Standards

- The contract

- Supervision notes

- The boundaries of confidentiality/sharing information

FUNCTIONS OF SUPERVISION

- Management

- Support

- Education

- Mediation

WHAT SHOULD BE IN A SUPERVISION CONTRACT

- Frequency

- Time

- Duration

- Location

- Format

- Setting the agenda

- Regular items for discussion

- Preparation for supervision sessions

- Recording of supervision sessions

- Boundaries of confidentiality

- Storage of notes

- Appraisals

- Review of contract

SUPERVISION ARRANGEMENTS

- **One to one**
  Manager or senior member of staff supervises one member of staff.

- **Paired**
  Manager or senior member of staff supervises two members of staff together.

- **Peer**
  Workers with the same level of responsibility supervise each other.

- **Group**
  Workers on the same level are supervised together in small groups with a senior person supervising.

- **Team**
  The whole staff group in a workplace are supervised together.

JOHN HERON'S SIX CATEGORIES OF HELPING INTERVENTIONS

Interventions can be **authoritative/directive**, i.e. the supervisor uses authority to be:

1. **Prescriptive**: gives advice, instruction

2. **Informative**: gives information

3. **Confrontative**: gives feedback, challenges

or **facilitative**, i.e. the supervisor values what the supervisee brings:

4. **Cathartic**: encourages expression of feelings

5. **Catalytic**: encourages reflection and problem-solving

6. **Supportive**: confirms, validates the individual.

(From: John Heron (1975) *Six Category Intervention Analysis.* Guildford: University of Surrey.)

CREATIVE SUPERVISION METHODS

- Discussion

- Rehearsal/role play/simulation

- Demonstration

- Modelling

- Shadowing

- Set tasks

- Exercises

Chapter 10

Dealing with Challenging Behaviour

'Challenging behaviour' is another term which has had increased usage in the past few years; unfortunately it is a term which is also used to label people – often incorrectly. This chapter will be concerned with how to deal with behaviours that are problematic for care workers. It is a huge subject on its own, and one which deserves the attention of a whole chapter. The reader should use this chapter in conjunction with Chapter 6 on risk assessment.

Violence towards staff is not acceptable

In July 1999 *Community Care* magazine launched its campaign *No Fear*, which aimed to raise awareness about the levels of violence towards all social care staff – this included both residential and fieldwork staff. Over the years many workers who have experienced violence and aggression from service users, have been told 'it's part of the job', 'it comes with the territory'. The expectation was that they should put up with it or get out. Fortunately, this attitude is changing, although it has not been wiped out completely. No worker should have to suffer violence and aggression from any service user. The dilemma for some workers is that they feel they cannot 'do anything' because the service user 'can't help it'.

As a result of the *Community Care* campaign the Government set up the National Task Force on Violence:

> The Government is determined to ensure that staff who spend their lives caring for others are not rewarded with intimidation and violence. 'Violence' means any incident where staff are abused, threatened or assaulted in circumstances related to their work, involving an explicit or implicit challenge to their safety, well-being or health. The definition is not subjective – it is what is meant by 'zero tolerance'. (DH 2000c, Resource Sheet 1)

What is challenging behaviour?

When the word 'violence' is used most people tend to think of physical attacks – hitting, slapping, stabbing, glassing – which cause grievous or actual bodily harm. But violence can be behaviour which causes psychological trauma; that is, emotional harm. As far back as the 1980s the Association of Directors of Social Services (ADSS) defined violence as:

> Behaviour which produces damaging or hurtful effects physically or emotionally on other people. (ADSS 1987)

In the 1990s the Health and Safety Executive England defined it as:

> Any incident in which a person is abused, threatened or assaulted in circumstances relating to their work. (Health and Safety Regulations Commission 1992)

It is good to have clear definitions but it is not enough. Organisations need to take responsibility to protect their workforces from violence and the culture within a workplace needs to be such that staff feel that they can report incidents and something will be done to support them. A worker should never feel guilty about reporting what has happened to them.

Some definitions of challenging behaviour are:

> Behaviour displayed by some people with LEARNING DISABILITY that is dangerous to themselves or other people, or is sufficiently unacceptable to significantly limit their opportunities for going out in public places. (Thomas and Pierson 1995, p.55)

> Challenging Behaviour is behaviour of such intensity, frequency or duration that the physical safety of the person or others is likely to be placed in serious jeopardy, or behaviour which is likely to seriously limit or delay access to and use of ordinary community facilities. (Emerson 2001, p.3)

When workers have worked in the social care field for a long time they may see some actions or behaviours as 'normal'. If the culture within a workplace has been that violence is part of the job and staff have not been encouraged to report when they have been a victim of violence, then it may be hard for those workers to think about what is not acceptable. It is useful for care workers to consider what behaviours are:

- understandable
- acceptable
- unacceptable.

Exercise 10.1 can be used as a starting point from which experienced workers can look back at what has happened to them in the past. Quiz Sheet 10.1 can also be used to focus workers on the issue of reporting.

Responsibilities

Organisations should value their staff and want to keep them. As employers they have a duty to promote health and safety at work. If workers are continuously victims of violence and aggression, they will either go off long term sick or leave the job.

Policies and procedures should be in place regarding dealing with violence and aggression. Staff need to have clear guidance on:

- definitions of violence and aggression

- what needs to be reported

- when to report

- who to report to.

A policy and procedure will usually include an incident form. Residential and day care staff are always telling me they spend so much of their time filling in these forms, but nothing ever happens. I have followed this up in some organisations and have found that it is often a paper exercise, which is absolutely pointless. Incident forms need to be properly audited. Where there is clearly a problem the organisation needs to take some action. Prior to this, a manager should be reading and responding to incident forms completed by workers. A good manager will interview and debrief a worker after an incident. This should include informing the worker of his/her rights and asking whether they want to take the matter further (e.g. contact the police). Some workers are horrified by this, but as the National Violence Task Force says:

> [Staff]…do not go to work to be victims of violence. Aggression, violence and threatening behaviour do not go with the job and will not be tolerated any longer. Individuals behaving violently towards staff will be reported to the police. (DH 2000c, Resource Sheet 1)

Workers should know *how* to report, but they should also feel comfortable in taking this action. Management has a responsibility to develop a culture whereby workers feel safe to do this. Where staff have been harmed, physically and/or emotionally, proper support should be offered. A manager should be able to give support but, in some situations, outside support may be needed in the form of counselling.

Some service users are placed in inappropriate settings. If this becomes evident, then a reassessment needs to be undertaken with a view to moving the person to another placement. The organisation's priority should not be about 'keeping bums in beds' (or chairs as in the case of day centres!).

Case study 10.1, p.306

So far the discussion has been about reacting to violence which has occurred. An organisation should be pro-active in trying to *prevent* violence and aggression. Strategies should be in place to reduce the risk of harm to staff. Part of this will be linked to providing adequate training. Workers need to understand what causes violence and aggression (theory) as well as knowing how to respond to it (methods).

Handout 10.1, p.300

Who presents challenging behaviour?

At the beginning of this chapter it was said that service users can be labelled as presenting challenging behaviour. Before saying someone is 'challenging' some work needs to be undertaken to find out what is causing the behaviour. This should be part of the risk assessment. It can be dangerous practice if the assessment only focuses on the present situation. It can be crucial to have an understanding of what has happened to the person in the past. But before exploring that further, we need to return to the subject of stereotyping.

Certain groups of service users are thought to be the ones who will be violent and aggressive. A typical example are people with mental health problems. Mental illness creates a lot of fear in some people because of the false image which often exists; that is, people who have mental health problems are going to commit acts of violence. The reality is that some will, the majority will not. Exercise 10.2 should bring out whether workers have a tendency to stereotype.

Care workers also need to be careful not to see problems where they do not exist. Some service users will have unpredictable mood swings. However, it is helpful to remember that we all have moods (some more than others) and these are affected by what has happened to us. A simple example is that a person who has had a bad day at work is not very likely to go home in a happy mood; they may be short-tempered, grumpy etc. On the other hand, if something really good has happened at work the person may go home full of energy and light-heartedness. This is the key to good practice – to find out what has happened to cause someone to behave in such a way. A care worker will not always understand what it is like to be a service user living in a home or attending a day centre.

Key Question

Is this behaviour understandable?

Reasons for challenging behaviour

There is no one simple theory to explain why a service user may present challenging behaviour. The causal factors could be numerous. This is why care workers need to take time to try to understand a service user and his/her behaviour. Some theorists believe that it is **innate** in humans to be aggressive in order to survive difficult situations. Others argue on **sociological** grounds that humans are influenced by society's norms, culture, role models, stereotyping etc.

There is a lot of emphasis nowadays on person-centred work and task-centred work. There is nothing wrong with adopting such methods of working, but the importance and relevance of past history should not be underestimated (that is, using the **psychodynamic approach**). What has happened to a person in the past is going to affect who they are today – their views, philosophy of life, how they behave. A person may behave differently when they are unexpectedly reminded of something from the past.

Case Example

Lydia had started to get slightly confused, but she remained the fairly happy-go-lucky person she had always been. Then, very suddenly, she started screaming and physically attacking a new service user, Arthur. In one of her lucid moments, Lydia was able to tell her keyworker that Arthur reminded her of her grandfather who had sexually abused her when she was a child.

The **behavioural** theorists would argue that if someone through their life has got their own way or what they wanted through violence and aggression then they will continue to use this behaviour.

Case Example

Helen had always been a strict disciplinarian. She talked a lot about how children today are not kept in control and that she believed a 'good slap with the belt never hurt anyone'. When service users with dementia wandered about or did not do what she or staff asked them immediately, Helen would intervene and be physically aggressive towards them.

Frustration theory explains challenging behaviour as a way in which a service user vents their anger.

Case Example

Ruby was partially sighted and the condition was getting worse. She started attending a day centre, but only went once a week so it was taking her a long time to get used to the environment. She kept bumping into chairs and tables. She got more and more frustrated as the weeks went on. She started shouting at the day centre workers and throwing objects (newspapers, dominoes, playing cards) at other service users.

Interactive theory argues that aggression breeds aggression.

Case Example

Albert was always shouting and swearing at service users and staff. One day an agency worker, Maddy, was in Albert's bedroom tidying up all the clothes he had pulled out of the wardrobe and drawers. It was nearing the end of the shift and Maddy was tired. When Albert started shouting at her, Maddy screamed back: 'For God's sake shut up will you?'

Some **medical conditions** can cause changes within a person. A good example is Alzheimer's disease. Family members can become very upset when someone's personality seems to change completely as well as their behaviour. Previously it was said that adults with mental health problems are stereotyped as being violent; certain mental illnesses may cause outbursts of violence. **Changes in medication** can also affect behaviour, as can the **intake or withdrawal of alcohol.**

The **environment** can also affect the mood and consequent behaviour of human beings. If service users are living in a dark and dingy environment where the furniture is old, the bedrooms small, and perhaps the service user feels hemmed in, they may become aggressive.

Handout 10.2, p.301

Case study 10.2, p.307

Managing challenging behaviour

There are two types of situation – predictable and unpredictable. There will be occasions when a service user has an outburst and care staff will be totally surprised by it. In these situations, workers have to think on their feet, but having had good basic training they should act in an appropriate manner. We have seen above that some service users will be known to present challenging behaviour. In these cases, workers need to undertake a risk assessment. By doing this, workers involved with the service user will have anticipated certain behaviours and developed a care plan which clearly stipulates how workers will respond; that is, what methods will be used.

It is not necessary to repeat what was written in Chapter 6 about risk assessment. It will suffice to say that workers must try to understand what might trigger off behaviours in order to protect other service users, workers and the general public from being harmed.

There are some common sense things which can be done to help prevent having to deal with challenging behaviour:

- Discuss with colleagues and professionals the challenging behaviour of a service user.

- Undertake a formal risk assessment.

- Do not be left alone with a service user who is known to be violent.

- Remove all dangerous objects.

- Think about wearing appropriate clothing and jewellery.

Handout 10.3, p.302

Case Example

Stacey was 18 years old and had come to work in the day centre to gain some experience of working with older people. She enjoyed buying clothes and was very 'fashion-conscious'. When she started work no one talked to her about appropriate clothing. During the first week she had to deal with service users who acted inappropriately towards her. One service user put his hand up her very short skirt. Stacey's ring scratched Laura's arm when she was toileting her; Laura reacted by pulling one of Stacey's large gipsy earrings from her ear.

Responding to challenging behaviour

It is not the purpose of this chapter to discuss all the different ways of responding to challenging behaviour. Care workers need thorough training on different methods; for example, breakaway techniques, acceptable restraint and so on. However, attention will be given to good practice points.

Care workers, like other social care staff, like to think that in a work situation they would respond appropriately and professionally. Everyone has their faults and weaknesses and it is important that these are dealt with on training courses. Care workers are likely to respond inappropriately when they are:

- tired

- frightened

- threatened

- lacking in confidence

- untrained.

Exercise 10.3 will help care workers to reflect on how they have dealt with situations in the past.

If a care worker feels that s/he is in a dangerous situation and could be harmed, then s/he should get out of the situation immediately. A worker should not feel obliged to stay and face every situation. Good practice points are:

- Assess the situation.

- Think before you act.

- Do not put yourself at risk of harm.

- Leave the situation if necessary.

- If staying in the situation try to defuse it.

Handout 10.4, p.303

If a care worker decides to deal with a situation s/he needs to think about:

- how s/he is perceived by the service user

- verbal responses

- body language.

Perception

A care worker may be perceived as a victim or an aggressor by what s/he says or does. We all do things which annoy other people – sometimes unwittingly. A care worker needs to be careful not to antagonise someone by their actions. For example, talking to a service user in a patronising way can make them feel angry. It can be things which are said that can inflame a situation or just the way a worker presents visually – like standing with hands on hips. It is important that the service user does not perceive the care worker as an aggressor or alternatively as a victim who s/he might play on.

Verbal responses

Some people are very good at making quick, clever comments, other people have a naturally vicious tongue. It is important when entering into dialogue with someone who is presenting challenging behaviour not to make them angry. Remaining calm but assertive is essential. A care worker should not get involved in a verbal battle; neither should s/he start raising their voice or shouting, nor threaten the service user or offer an ultimatum. Words and phrases need to be chosen carefully; that is, a care worker should not seem as though they are talking like a parent or schoolteacher to a child – for example, saying 'Don't do that or else…'. Certain cliches or jargon can just alienate the service user further – for example, 'I know where you're coming from'; 'I understand how you must be feeling'; 'We'll talk it through.'

Body language

Much has already been written about body language in Chapter 7 and the reader should revisit that chapter. Key points to remember are:

- Think about your positioning – do not stand right opposite the service user as this may seem confrontational; stand at a slight angle.

- If you feel safe enough, you should sit down with the service user – on the same level.

- Do not get too close – maintain three feet between you and the service user whether standing or sitting.

- Only use touch if you are sure it is safe and appropriate to do so.

- Maintain eye contact.

- Do not cross your arms or legs.

- Do not use jerky hand or leg movements (which could be seen as aggressive or threatening).

- Do not point.

Handout 10.5, p.304

Case study 10.3, p.308

Use of restraint

The whole subject of using restraint is a real hot potato. Any form of restraint should be a last resort. The reality is that some service users are a danger either to themselves, other service users, staff or the general public and where there is high risk some form of restraint may have to be used. However, before agreeing to any form of restraint, all the professionals involved with the service user must be consulted in relation to undertaking a risk assessment. In some cases it will be necessary to take advice from and include solicitors and police in the process.

There can be different forms of restraint:

- physical
- chemical.

Care staff attending Counsel and Care seminars said the following could be deemed as restraint:

- Using furniture to 'protect' people from falling
- Locking people up
- Using cot sides or bed rails
- Restricting freedom of movement
- Using mechanical aids to make up for lack of staff – buzzers, alarms, locks
- Removing walking aids
- Using drugs to control behaviour
- Restricting social contact and time of contact
- Removing call buzzer.

(Clarke and Bright 2002, p.4)

Exercise 10.4 will encourage care workers to think about whether they use restraint – consciously or unconsciously – in their workplace.

Exercises

Exercise 10.5, Handout 10.6 and Role Plays 10.1 and 10.2 will help care workers anticipate how they might deal with certain situations.

☺ **ROLE PLAY 10.1**

Care worker:

You are in the bathroom with Joyce, who has Alzheimer's disease. Bathing Joyce is always problematic because she says she does not like people touching her. Joyce has had epileptic fits in the past and needs to be watched carefully. You are trying to encourage Joyce to get undressed but she starts throwing things (e.g. towels, soap, shampoo bottle) at you.

Joyce:

You have Alzheimer's disease. You hate being bathed because you do not like people seeing you naked. You become very aggressive when the care worker tries to encourage you to get undressed. You start throwing things at her/him (e.g. towels, soap, shampoo bottle etc.).

☺ **ROLE PLAY 10.2**

Day centre worker:

A new service user, Roger, has come to the day centre today. He is not talking to anybody else and has refused to participate in any of the activities. He has sworn a few times at the women. You are now taking him into the office to have a private word with him.

Roger:

It is your first day at the day centre. You did not want to come but your daughter forced you into it, so you've done it to please her. You are venting your anger now towards other service users. You have refused to talk to anybody else, except to swear at the women. A care worker has now brought you into the office to talk to you. You are going to be aggressive verbally, but also act in a way so that s/he feels physically threatened.

Suggested reading

Braithwaite, R. (2001) *Managing Aggression.* London: Routledge.

Clarke, A. and Bright, L. (2002) *Showing Restraint: Challenging the Use of Restraint in Care Homes.* London: Counsel and Care.

Counsel and Care (2002) *Residents Taking Risks: Minimising the Use of Restraint – A Guide for Care Homes.* London: Counsel and Care.

Department of Health (2000c) *We Don't Have To Take This* Resource Pack. London: Department of Health.

Department of Health (2001a) *A Safer Place: Combating Violence Against Social Care Staff.* London: Department of Health.

Goldsmith, M. (1996) *Hearing the Voice of People with Dementia.* London: Jessica Kingsley Publishers. Chapter 11 'Challenging Behaviour.'

Holden, U. and Chapman, A. (1994) *'Wait A Minute!' – A Practice Guide on Challenging Behaviour and Aggression for Staff Working with Individuals Who Have Dementia.* Stirling: Dementia Services Development Centre.

Useful website

Department of Health – Violence Task Force: www.doh.gov.uk/violencetaskforce

🎞 VIDEO

Managing Challenging Behaviour

WHAT HAS HAPPENED TO YOU?

Objective

To get care workers to share their experiences of violence and aggression.

Participants

Small groups.

Equipment

Flipchart paper and pens.

Time

20 minutes.

Task

1. Participants discuss incidents where they have been victims of violence and aggression.

2. List types of behaviour – what had actually happened.

3. Beside each behaviour write whether it was (i) understandable, (ii) acceptable, (iii) unacceptable.

4. Put ticks by the behaviours which were reported.

Feedback

1. Each group presents their lists.

2. Trainer draws discussion about incidents listed which were not reported and asks whether participants now think they should have been reported.

WHO IS VIOLENT?

Objective

To get care workers to admit that they sometimes label and stereotype people.

Participants

Large group.

Equipment

Flipchart stand, paper and pens.

Time

15 minutes.

Task

The trainer asks participants to be honest when answering the questions:

1. Which service user groups do you expect to present violence and aggression?

2. Are some groups more likely to present challenging behaviour than others?

3. Open discussion.

WHAT DID YOU DO?

Objective

For care workers to highlight their weaknesses.

Participants

Small groups.

Equipment

Flipchart paper and pens.

Time

15 minute discussion.

Task

1. Think of a time when you have felt threatened – either in a work or personal situation.

2. Discuss in the group:

    (a) What you did.

    (b) Did you handle the situation well or badly?

    (c) With hindsight what would you have done differently?

3. Make a list of good practice tips on the flipchart sheet.

Feedback

1. Each group will feed back their good practice tips.

2. Open discussion will follow where more tips can be added.

3. The lists will be typed up and given to participants after the course.

DO YOU USE RESTRAINT?

Objective

For care workers to think about whether they restrain their service users in any way – consciously or unconsciously.

Participants

Small groups – preferably staff groups from the same home or day centre working together.

Equipment

Flipchart paper and pens.

Time

15 minutes.

Task

1. Think about the service users you work with. Do you have to restrain any of them and what is the reason for this?

2. Is the method of restraint written in the care plan?

3. What types of restraint do you use?

4. Do you now think you restrain service users, when prior to this exercise you might not have thought what you did as being a form of restraint?

Feedback

1. Each group discusses types of restraint used in their workplace.

2. Trainer facilitates discussion about acceptable and unacceptable forms of restraint.

WHAT WOULD YOU DO IF...?

Objective

For care workers to anticipate how they would respond to challenging behaviour.

Participants

Small groups.

Equipment

Flipchart paper and pens.
Photocopies of Handout 10.6.

Time

25 minutes.

Task

1. You are asked to read and think about the 5 scenarios on Handout 10.6.

2. Consider each scenario in turn. Discuss in your group what you would say and do to the people involved.

3. Would you report the incident? If so, to whom?

Feedback

1. Each group will feed back their answers.

2. Large group discussion on comparing responses and strategies employed.

QUIZ SHEET 10.1

Would you report (either by telling your Manager or completing an incident form) that a service user had:

1. Told You to 'Piss off'?   Yes/No/Don't know

2. Shouted and screamed at you?   Yes/No/Don't know

3. Called You a 'bitch' or 'bastard'?   Yes/No/Don't know

4. Slapped you across the face?   Yes/No/Don't know

5. Poked you in the eye?   Yes/No/Don't know

6. Pulled your hair?   Yes/No/Don't know

7. Spat at you?   Yes/No/Don't know

8. Bent your fingers backwards/
   forwards?   Yes/No/Don't know

9. Pinched you?   Yes/No/Don't know

10. Bitten you?   Yes/No/Don't know

11. Scratched you with their nails?   Yes/No/Don't know

12. Cut you with nail scissors?   Yes/No/Don't know

13. Smeared faeces on you?   Yes/No/Don't know

14. Hit your bottom with a walking stick/belt?   Yes/No/Don't know

15. Squeezed your breasts/genitals?   Yes/No/Don't know

16. Thrown a plate at you in the dining room?   Yes/No/Don't know

17. Burnt you with a cigarette?   Yes/No/Don't know

18. Threatened you with a knife?   Yes/No/Don't know

19. Held you against a wall?   Yes/No/Don't know

20. Held your arm behind your back?   Yes/No/Don't know

WHAT SHOULD BE IN PLACE

- Policy and procedure on violence in the workplace

- Strategy for reducing violence and aggression to workers

- Related policies and procedures, e.g. risk assessment, harassment, bullying

- Training on managing violence and aggression

- Incident form

- Auditing procedure

- Debriefing procedure

- Culture which supports staff to report

- Practical support and counselling for staff

THEORIES REGARDING AGGRESSION AND VIOLENCE

- Innate/genetic

- Sociological

- Psychodynamic

- Behavioural

- Frustration

- Interactive

- Environmental

- Medical conditions

- Changes in medication

- Intake/withdrawal of alcohol, drugs

PREVENTION

A care worker can do the following things as a way of undertaking preventative work:

- Discuss with colleagues and professionals the challenging behaviour of a service user

- Undertake a formal risk assessment

- Do not be left alone with a service user who is known to be violent

- Remove all dangerous objects

- Think about wearing appropriate clothing and jewellery

GOOD PRACTICE POINTS FOR DEALING WITH VIOLENCE/AGGRESSION

- Assess the situation

- Think before you act

- Do not put yourself at risk of harm

- Leave the situation if necessary

- If staying in the situation try to defuse it

WHEN RESPONDING TO CHALLENGING BEHAVIOUR THINK ABOUT:

- Positioning

- Space

- Use of touch

- Use of words

- Maintaining eye contact

- Keeping an open position

- Not using jerky or sudden movements and not pointing

WHAT WOULD YOU DO IF...?

1. Richard is schizophrenic; most of the time he is fine when he attends day centre. However, when he decides to stop taking his medication he can become aggressive. Today he is eating his lunch; three other service users are at the table with him. An argument breaks out between Richard and Alan, another service user who has dementia. Richard stands up and is threatening to hit Alan with the water jug. Alan picks up a knife.

2. Beatrice and Jennifer are two service users who have never liked each other. You're walking along the corridor; a bathroom door is open and as you look in you see that Beatrice has Jennifer's head down the toilet.

3. Donovan has just come to live in the residential home. He presents as being very bad tempered and has been seen throwing things. Another service user tells you Donovan has just spat on him.

4. You hear someone shouting for help from the medical room. You rush in to find that a male service user has the district nurse pinned down on the floor.

5. A service user with learning disabilities throws a radio through the window. She then picks up pieces of broken glass and starts throwing them across the lounge where other service users are sitting.

Case Study 10.1

Maxine, who had profound learning disabilities, was living in residential care with six other service users. Staff were finding it very hard to manage her behaviour; she was violent both to staff and the other service users. Staff reported every incident to the manager and the difficulties were raised at every team meeting. All the care workers felt ill-equipped to deal with Maxine's behaviour but they also believed the staffing levels were too low. The manager was unsympathetic and said: 'If you can't hack it, then go and work somewhere else.' Sickness levels of staff increased. No action was taken until Maxine stabbed a worker in the stomach with a pair of scissors.

Discuss

1. If you had been one of the workers who was supporting Maxine, how would you have responded verbally when the manager said 'If you can't hack it, then go and work somewhere else'?

2. What else might you have done when the manager refused to take any action?

Case Study 10.2

Seth has always made it known that he likes a drink. When he first came into the home it was made clear to him that excessive drinking would not be tolerated. Other professionals who had previously been involved with Seth told the social worker that he had abused alcohol most of his life. The consultant at the local hospital treated Seth for liver damage some years ago. Every Friday night Seth's friend Jack comes to visit. Staff suspect that Jack brings drink in for Seth but there is never any physical evidence of this. Seth becomes very loud when he has been drinking and in recent weeks this has become more evident. He totally denies that he has been drinking. You and a colleague are on duty tonight. It is 11.30p.m. You hear crashing and banging about from upstairs. You both run upstairs and find Seth wandering along the corridor banging on doors and opening them; he is being verbally abusive to service users in their rooms. He is carrying a walking stick in his hand. When he sees the two of you he tells you to keep away from him and threatens that he will 'give you a good thrashing'.

Discuss

1. What would you do in this situation?
2. Do you think something should have been done before this incident? If so, what exactly?
3. When this incident is over, what should you do?
4. What support should be offered to you and your colleague?

Case Study 10.3

St Philip's Day Centre is run for older people with dementia. Pauline Sadler is 75 years old and has a tendency to pick up things and hit objects and sometimes people. Staff have felt able to manage the behaviour but have acknowledged that it is becoming worse. Unfortunately, a new service user, Stella, has taken to copying Pauline's behaviour. Today, Pauline is being more aggressive than usual. She has been throwing things across the room and shouting and swearing at other service users. Stella has been joining in but because she is younger and more mobile than Pauline she has got up and hit two other service users on the head with a tray.

Discuss

1. What would you do immediately to deal with this situation?

2. What should happen after you have defused this situation? Think in terms of (i) the staff (ii) Pauline and Stella (iii) the other service users.

3. What do you think should happen in regard to risk assessment and care planning for Pauline?

4. What do you think should happen in regard to risk assessment and care planning for Stella?

Chapter 11

Death, Dying and Bereavement

Information in this chapter is relevant to:

TRAINING ORGANISATION for the PERSONAL SOCIAL SERVICES

TOPSS Induction Standard 3 – Understand the experiences and the particular needs of the service user groups

3.2.4   Understand how to respond to death, dying and bereavement

NATIONAL VOCATIONAL QUALIFICATIONS

NC1   Enable individuals, their family and friends to adjust to and manage their loss

NC3   Support individuals and others through the process of dying

The subject of death, dying and bereavement is just one part of TOPSS Induction Standard 3, but deserves a chapter of this manual to be devoted to it. Care workers who work with older people are going to have to deal with death and dying as an integral part of their job. Deaths will occur in homes on a fairly regular basis, but day centre workers will also lose service users. Care workers need training on how to support someone who is facing death; some service users will want to die in the home and these wishes should be supported if the home has the necessary facilities to do this. Again day care workers may face the same task; a service user may continue to use day care whilst they are terminally ill. Bereavement is a linked subject area. Care workers will have to deal with the grief of others but will have to come to terms with their own losses as well.

When training staff on this subject, a trainer must be conscious of the fact that some workers will never have experienced a death, whereas others may be very used to dealing with death and dying. It is a very sensitive subject and a trainer must be ready to deal with all the emotions which may be unleashed during training. It is vital that time and space is given to talk in depth about feelings, including fears.

It is helpful for a manager to find out what is available for training on a local level. Many funeral directors provide training in the form of visits to their offices so that workers can learn about what actually happens to the body and services which can be offered; some crematoriums also arrange visits.

Before talking about death and dying, it is important to give some attention to the topic of loss, which is linked to death and dying, but deserves discussion as a separate subject area.

Loss

Loss is something which everyone has experienced at some point in their life. We all will have lost something which is of special importance to us; for example:

- through a burglary, an object which was of sentimental value and can never be replaced
- a person when a relationship finishes
- a child when they leave home permanently
- a job when redundancies occur.

Older people will have experienced losses through their lives and are likely to experience even more as they approach later adulthood. Much has been written about facing unresolved issues before death and care workers should be made aware of this, so that they can undertake this area of work if it is an issue for someone (Hunt, Marshall and Rowlings 1997; Pritchard 2000). Mortality rates were much higher years ago and some older people may have lived through both World Wars, so they will have experienced the loss of parents, siblings, spouses, friends. In the past it was 'normal' to hide your feelings – the 'stiff upper lip' syndrome; people were not encouraged to show their feelings or grief. Therefore, some older people need the opportunity to grieve now – no matter how many years have passed since the loss.

Those who have experienced abuse and neglect may feel that they lost other things; for example, their childhood, freedom, dignity, opportunities, relationships etc. Strategies can be developed through life to cope with situations and to outsiders it may seem that someone is dealing with life successfully. However, on the inside the person may be experiencing all sorts of emotions and there may be a need to voice these feelings before they die.

Physical and mental losses (and the effect on ability to do things) can be experienced at any time in life, but an older person who suffers ill-health may experience more in later life:

- sight
- hearing
- speech
- mobility
- mental capacity.

As people grow older they may have to adjust to a lot of changes because of loss of:

- employment
- income.

When an older person is admitted to a home permanently, s/he may feel that they are losing their:

- own home
- space
- belongings

- identity
- freedom
- independence.

Care workers should find out how the person really feels about admission to care. They may have accepted it reluctantly and be blaming other people for their situation. Even if they have been happy to come into care they will have certain fears or anxieties which need to be expressed and dealt with.

Care workers in homes and day centres need to identify any losses the service user has not come to terms with, no matter what they relate to (past or present), and to help them to work through the loss and their feelings. It is a very important piece of work which needs to be undertaken.

Exercise 11.1 will help care workers to consider how they have dealt with their own losses in life.

The subject of death

Earlier in the manual mention was made of how some people might fear getting old; a lot of this stems from people having negative images about old age. Death can also evoke fear and avoidance. Most people do not want to die, but pain and death are often linked together. Death can be a happy release for some people. For those who have religious beliefs, death is a passage to a better life and is welcomed.

Care workers must be given the opportunity to talk about the subject of death and the myths surrounding it. Early on in any training course on death and dying, feelings about the subject of death must be vented. Exercise 11.2 will facilitate this.

Care workers and death

A care worker might have to deal with death both in their working life and in their personal life. They may experience the death of:

- service user
- colleague
- family member
- friend
- someone close to a service user.

Experience of death

When training on death and dying it is important to alert course participants that the course content is emotive and that some of them might be affected by it. If a formal course is being arranged, then the flyer advertising the course should include this warning note. If a manager is inducting staff then again some kind of warning is necessary and ground rules should be set so that a worker can take time out from the training if necessary. If a worker does become upset support must be given to that person. A manager should always take steps to find out if any course is going to affect a worker because of their own personal experience. For example, if a worker has experienced a death of a close friend or relative recently, having to train on the subject is going to be very hard for them. I believe that in some cases there should be some flexibility regarding participation; that is, it may not be the right time for a care worker to attend the course. This is something which should be addressed in supervision. For more discussion on preparation for trainers see Chapter 4 in Pritchard (2001a).

When training on death and dying, workers must be encouraged (not forced) to talk about their own experiences. There will be workers who have never experienced the death of anyone close to them; others will never have been to a funeral; and others will never have seen a dead body. At an early stage in the training it is important to find out what fears workers have regarding death and dying. Exercise 11.3 will facilitate this.

Death and the care plan

One of the topics with must be addressed in a care plan is death and dying. A care worker might feel uncomfortable raising this topic of conversation when someone has just been admitted to care, but it has to be done. The care plan needs to include details of any special arrangements or wishes the service user may have regarding dying and funeral arrangements. Service users can die suddenly or some will have no family or relatives, so it is important to know whether they want to be buried or cremated.

☺ **ROLE PLAY 11.1**

Care worker:

Mrs Rose was admitted to care a few days ago. You are going to be her keyworker. You have been off work for a few days and are now going to meet her. Some of the care plan has been completed – mainly the basic details. You need to raise the issue of funeral arrangements and to find out if she has any particular wishes.

Mrs Rose:

You came to live in the home a few days ago. You have met a lot of staff but only today are you going to meet your keyworker, because she has been off for a few days. All you know is that she needs to talk to you about the care plan.

How death happens

Death can happen in all sorts of ways and whenever it occurs it will still be hard for those who are left to deal with it. A new care worker who is coming to work in a home or day centre might think death will come in the form of older people dying of illnesses. This will happen, but care workers need to think about what else might transpire. Death can be sudden or expected. There will be deaths which are caused in extraordinary circumstances, which most people do not think are common and certainly do not want to think about – like murder.

Then there is suicide, which is still a taboo subject for some people. Older people will remember that not so long ago people who committed suicide were not allowed to be buried in consecrated ground. Shame and embarrassment might still be a common reaction to suicide. In 2000, there were 6399 suicides in the United Kingdom and the Republic of Ireland, of which 75 per cent were by men. Older people have a relatively high rate of suicide compared with the general population. In 1999, 16 per cent of all suicides were people aged over 64 years (The Samaritans 2002).

Exercise 11.4 is designed to help care workers think about how they might support someone on hearing the news of a death.

Working with and supporting someone who is dying

Some service users will know that they are going to die in the near future. Some will just have a feeling that death is imminent; they might share this with somebody or keep it to themselves and get on with making their own preparations. Others will be told that they have a terminal illness. When a service user knows they are dying they will need physical and emotional support from people around them. A care worker's role will be to check out with the person what they want to happen. Key questions will be about:

- where to die?

- visitors – who to see/not see?

- information sharing – who should be kept informed? Should any information be withheld?

- special comforts – to have certain music playing; to be read to etc.

- who should be there at the end?

- funeral arrangements.

Handout 11.2, p.331

If someone is terminally ill and wants to die in the home, staff must assess whether they have the facilities and skills to provide the proper care or whether this can be achieved with help from outside (e.g. GP, Macmillan nurses). Care workers need to seek help and advice from professionals about the progression of diseases, conditions etc. As was suggested earlier in the manual, there are many organisations which can provide useful information and leaflets about certain illnesses (see Appendix 2).

No one can ever be accurate about how long someone has to live. It is dangerous to cling on to any time limits that have been specified. However, care workers need to be aware about the stages of dying that a terminally ill person might go through. If workers are to support service users who are dying, then they must be trained in this in order to have an understanding of the emotions which may be presented.

Kubler-Ross (1995) has written about the stages of facing death being:

1. Denial and isolation (usually occurs after a person is told they are terminally ill)

2. Anger (replaces denial and will be vented at random – towards doctors, family, care staff, other service users)

3.   Bargaining (person tries to make an agreement in order to get more time)

4.   Depression (person is no longer in denial or angry but will feel a great sense of loss)

5.   Acceptance (the anger and struggle to accept the inevitable have gone).

📑 Handout 11.3, p.332

In this day and age, we are all encouraged to vent our feelings in order to deal with things. This applies to people who are facing death; it is thought they should talk about how they feel and plan for their death. Some people will do this with the right support. However, there will always be those older people who will keep their feelings to themselves; some will also remain in denial for most of the time. The role of the care worker is to offer the opportunity to talk. Some workers may feel scared about doing this because they do not believe that they have the necessary skills. Care workers are not required to become fully qualified counsellors. Helping someone through the dying process is about listening and responding to them. Sometimes it is much easier for a dying person to talk to someone outside the family or circle of friends, because the dying person may be frightened of upsetting people close to them. The person may wish to talk about:

- past life
- regrets
- secrets
- unresolved issues
- how they can put certain things right
- feelings
- fears
- hopes
- dying
- the end
- after death
- the funeral.

📑 Handout 11.4, p.333

Case Example

Mr Miller was dying of cancer and was bedridden. He had very set ideas about what he wanted to happen at his funeral and that was well planned out with care staff. He became quite obsessional about what he wanted to be buried in and definitely did not want a traditional wooden coffin. He asked his keyworker to go to the local funeral director's to get some brochures, so he could 'choose my own box'. He spent hours looking at the brochures and eventually decided on a lead casket which was black with silver trimming and handles and pure white lining inside. He also got his keyworker to go out to buy a new suit and shoes to be buried in.

The death

Preparing for the actual death is important. One can never predict what it is going to be like; some people will be unconscious for days before the end; others may be talking right up to point of death. Care workers need to know what will make the person feel most comfortable – for example, do they want quiet/silence; music; readings; people around them; a spiritual leader?

It is necessary to know if someone follows a particular religion and whether certain rituals need to be followed. This is very important when a service user is from a different ethnic group. Care staff need to find out about what they can and cannot do. In some cultures, the dead body should not be touched by anyone outside of the religion.

Case Example

Vijay Amin was a very religious Hindu man, who was determined not to die in hospital. His family had set up a shrine in his room and when they were called into the home when the end was near, they brought a priest with them. Prayers were read from the Bhagavad Gita (Holy Book) after Vijay had asked to be placed on the floor.

Immediately after the death, care workers should think about:

- informing necessary people e.g. GP (to certify death), relatives, friends
- giving relatives/friends enough time with the body – not rushing them
- attending the body (this may need to be done by the family/religious members)
- making arrangements for the body to be moved (contacting funeral director)
- whether a funeral has to take place within certain time limits (for a particular religion)
- whether a period of mourning is required.

Handout 11.5, p.334

If a care worker has never seen a dead body it is important for them to be trained on what happens to the body after death and what needs to be attended to. A doctor or a funeral director can provide such information.

Deaths outside the home/day centre

Some service users will die in hospital or in a hospice. If they have left friends behind in the home or day centre, they will probably be anxious to hear about what is happening.

The role of the care worker is to find out about the current situation and keep people informed. If at all possible, care staff should try to visit the dying service user to give them continuing support and it may be possible to arrange for other service users to visit as well.

Care workers should never be over-protective towards older people. Sometimes it is thought death should be kept from them because it will remind them of their own mortality. Most older people know that death is not so far away. Families and friends think hiding things from older relatives is the best thing to do. This is a piece of work a care worker can undertake in the care plan; that is, discuss with the service user how they would like to be treated, kept informed etc.

Case Example

James was very angry when he was told by his family that his grand-daughter, Amy, had died a few days ago. Amy was 10 years old and had had leukaemia for the past 7 years. The family had not told James that she had been ill again; he thought she was still in remission. James was furious that he had not been able to say 'goodbye' to Amy. The family said they thought he would have been too upset if he had known the truth.

Service users also form important relationships within a day centre. Therefore, if a service user is ill and does not attend staff should make the effort to find out what is happening to them and keep the other service users informed if they wish to know (obviously with the permission of the service user who is ill/dying). Maintaining relationships and support is crucial.

Announcing the death

This follows on from what has already been said. Older people need to be kept informed. If a service user has died in the home, it should not be kept a secret. Care staff should be open and honest about when it happened. Similarly, in a day centre if a service user has died an announcement needs to be made.

It is important for both service users and staff to be able to deal with the death by talking about it. Judgements have to be made on how to make the announcement. Sometimes it may be deemed appropriate to announce it when service users are together – in the lounge or dining room. Or maybe individuals need to be told separately – especially if they were particularly close to the person who has died.

Some service users will want to pay their respects. Some may wish to:

- view the body

- say a prayer

- have a minute's silence

- light a candle.

Managers and care staff must try to remember if anyone is absent when a death occurs. There is nothing worse than a care worker returning to work after a few days off or a holiday and finding out by accident that a service user has died. The same is true if a service user has been in hospital and returns to the home to find a friend has passed away.

The funeral

Funerals are a way of saying 'goodbye' to the dead person. Some people find them comforting, others dread them. The purpose of a funeral will differ according to religion; some will see it as primarily for the mourners, others for the deceased person and the passage of their soul.

A care worker in a home will have undertaken some work to find out what sort of funeral is going to take place. Again it needs to be emphasised that customs and rituals may differ for different religions. Care workers should find out about this in advance for themselves and also for other service users who want to attend the funeral.

Case Example

Mr Stirling was African-Caribbean and had been well liked by both staff and service users; quite a few of them wanted to attend his funeral. Mr Stirling was a Seventh Day Adventist. Two care workers accompanied the service users to the funeral. They were all shocked when they followed the other mourners around the coffin; they had not expected it to be open.

Bereavement

When talking about bereavement it is important to repeat a principle which has been evident throughout this manual – everyone is an individual and will handle situations differently. However, much has been written about the four stages of grief:

1. Shock and disbelief (the person may say they feel numb; they are failing to accept the loss)

2. Expressions of grief (shows acute anxiety, pines for the dead person, remembers the good times)

3. Depression and apathy (becomes irritable, feels despair, a sense of hopelessness and disorganisation)

4. Signs of recovery (reorganises life).

Handout 11.6, p.335

The immediate reaction after someone has died is to experience numbness. The stages which follow may occur at different times and very often bereaved people do not follow a set pattern through these stages. A care worker may be required to support a number of people through bereavement; this could be:

- service users

- family and friends of the service user who has died

- colleagues

- other professionals/workers who were involved with the service user who has died.

If a care worker has not experienced a death before s/he may feel very uncomfortable: 'I don't know what to say.' It is important not to use cliches, for example 'Time is a great healer', or to avoid talking about the dead person. CRUSE have a very useful booklet entitled *Has Someone Died?*, which includes comments from bereaved people about what was helpful and unhelpful to them. Staff may be required to give ongoing support to relatives, who might find comfort in keeping contact with people who knew their relative. Exercise 11.5 should help care workers to think how they were helped during times of losses and bereavement.

😐 ROLE PLAY 11.2

Day care worker:

Edna has arrived at day centre very upset. The escort on the bus has told you very quickly that one of her three daughters died last Saturday, but you do not know which one. Edna is sitting down and sobbing. You need to go to talk to her.

Edna:

You have just arrived at day centre and you are sobbing uncontrollably. Your eldest daughter Margaret (you have three daughters) died suddenly last Saturday. She had a heart attack in the supermarket and died later in hospital. She was only 58 years old. There has been a delay with the funeral, which will not take place until next week. You wanted to come to day centre to take your mind off things for a while. You told the transport people that one of your daughters died, but now you have got to the centre you can't stop crying.

😐 ROLE PLAY 11.3

Day care worker:

Fred and Lizzie Copeland used to come to day centre together. Lizzie then became ill with cancer and was told she was terminally ill. Fred has continued to come to day centre once a week. Last week he told you that Lizzie had gone into the hospice. You are now going to talk to Fred about what has happened since you saw him last week.

Fred Copeland:

You attend day centre once a week. Your wife, Lizzie, is terminally ill with cancer; you used to come to day centre together. Lizzie went into the hospice last week and it looks like she will die within the next few days. You wanted to come to the centre today so that you can talk about Lizzie, because the day care workers know her so well. You do not feel you can talk in the same way to the hospice workers.

Importance of anniversaries

Care workers need to be conscious of when anniversaries are due; this is something which should be included in a care plan in order to remember significant dates. Service users who have lost somebody may wish to visit the grave or crematorium on the anniversary of the death. Leading up to the anniversary the bereaved person may experience depression and their behaviour may change slightly. Staff need to be aware of this and not think that something else is happening.

Support for staff

So far the discussion has been about supporting service users and people connected to them. Some mention must be made about the support staff need. One never gets used to death to the degree that it has no effect at all on you. Everyone needs to express their grief in some way. A manager is going to deal with all sorts of situations regarding staff; some will be new to dealing with the death of a service user; others may be very experienced but have perhaps got too involved with a service user.

Care staff are encouraged to be professional; this does not mean that they should bottle up all their feelings. They should remain in control while dealing with service users and family related to the deceased person, but they must be able to vent their feelings (like having a good cry) in an appropriate place; for example, the office or staff room. Any induction course should include training about personal involvement and professional boundaries. This is a very hard thing to maintain when you have worked with someone for a long time, but it is important to keep a professional distance. Service users should never be seen to be 'like family' and the care worker should never be seen to be out of control with their emotions. Staff should be given time and space to:

- talk about their feelings

- show their feelings

- deal with the loss and grief.

Suggested reading

Counsel and Care (1995) *Last Rights*. London: Counsel and Care.

Cruse Bereavement Care *Has Someone Died?* London: CRUSE.

Hunt, L., Marshall, M. and Rowlings, C. (1997) *Past Trauma in Late Life*. London: Jessica Kingsley Publishers.

Kubler-Ross, E. (1995) *On Death and Dying*. London: Routledge.

Neuberger, J. (1994) *Caring for Dying People of Different Faiths*. London: Mosby.

Parkes, C.M. and Markus, A. (1998) *Coping with Loss*. London: BMJ Books.

Scrutton, S. (1995) *Bereavement and Grief: Supporting Older People Through Loss*. London: Edward Arnold.

Smith, P. (1998) *Death and Dying in a Nursing Home*. Norwich: Social Work Monographs.

Thompson, N. (2002) *Loss and Grief: A Guide for Human Services Practitioners*. Basingstoke: Palgrave.

Useful organisation

Cruse Bereavement Care

Cruse House, 126 Sheen Road, Richmond, Surrey TW9 1UR

Tel: 020 8939 9530 Fax: 020 8940 7638 Helpline: 0870 167 1677

E-mail: info@crusebereavementcare.org.uk

Website: www.crusebereavementcare.org.uk

VIDEOS

Death, Dying and Bereavement

Needs of the Service User

DEALING WITH LOSSES

Objective

For care workers to consider how they have dealt with their own losses in life.

Participants

Individual and small group work.

Equipment

Flipchart paper and pens.

Time

25 minutes.

Task

1. Each participant is asked to think about one major loss they have experienced in their life.

2. In groups discuss:

   - How you felt at the time of the loss.

   - What effect did it have on your behaviour?

   - How did you cope?

   - What was helpful to you?

   - What was unhelpful to you?

Feedback

1. Each group will feed back key points from their discussions.

2. Trainer will make a list of coping strategies, which can be typed up after the course and circulated to participants.

DEATH: WORD ASSOCIATION

Objective

To understand how care workers perceive death.

Participants

Large group exercise.

Equipment

Flipchart stand, paper and pens.

Time

30 minutes for discussion.

Task

1. Trainer asks the group to focus on the word 'death' and what comes into mind when they hear the word.

2. Trainer lists the key points from the reactions.

3. The trainer will then facilitate discussion about how death is perceived by other people (different age groups, different cultures, religions etc.).

FEARS REGARDING WORKING WITH DEATH AND DYING

Objective

For care workers to vent fears regarding death and dying.

Participants

Participants will work in pairs – with someone they feel comfortable with.

Equipment

Paper and pens.

Time

10 minutes in pairs; 15 minutes to share with another pair.

Task

1. The pairs will discuss what they fear about death itself and the possibility of working with death.

2. They will make a list of their fears.

3. They will then share their list with another pair.

Feedback

1. The groups of 4 will feed back their common fears.

2. Open discussion.

HEARING ABOUT A DEATH: GIVING SUPPORT

Objective

For care workers to think about how they would react on hearing the news of someone's death.

Participants

Small groups.

Equipment

Trainer will have photocopied Handout 11.1.
Flipchart paper and pens.

Time

30 minutes.

Tasks

1. Discuss what you would say and do for each scenario on Handout 11.1.

2. Write the actual responses in sentences on the flipchart sheet.

3. Write actions under a separate heading on the flipchart sheet.

Feedback

1. Trainer leads by taking one scenario at a time and getting feedback from each group.

2. Open discussion on appropriate responses.

BEING COMFORTED

Objective

To get care workers to think about what was helpful to them when they suffered a loss or bereavement.

Participants

Small groups.

Equipment

Flipchart paper and pens.

Time

20 minutes.

Task

1. Participants are asked to think of a time in their life when they have suffered a loss or bereavement. (This can be linked back to Exercise 11.1 if required.)

2. Participants are asked to discuss:

   - Who supported you through this loss?

   - What was helpful?

   - What was unhelpful?

   - Was there anything else that would have helped you?

   - What do you need to happen when you are upset?

3. Participants write down the key points from the discussion for each question.

Feedback

1. Groups feed back their work.

2. Trainer makes a list of possible strategies for supporting a bereaved person. This list will be typed up after the course and circulated to participants.

HEARING ABOUT A DEATH: GIVING SUPPORT

Residential settings

1. Bill was using the telephone in the hallway and became very upset. He went straight up to his bedroom after the conversation had ended. You have come to check on him. He tells you he has just learnt that his brother has committed suicide.

2. You have to tell a service user, Maisie, that another service user, Esther, died in her sleep last night. Maisie and Esther have been close friends in the home for years.

3. You and another care worker (who is also your friend outside work), Judy, are having a break. The manager comes in and says she needs a word with Judy in the office; she suggests you come in with her. The manager tells Judy that her husband has been killed in a car crash.

4. Terence has been ill for a long time; he said he wanted to die in the home rather than hospital. All the service users know that the death is imminent. Terence has died this morning. You have to tell the service users.

5. A colleague was stabbed to death outside a nightclub over the weekend. The manager has just informed the staff and now the service users need to know.

Day care settings

1. You arrive at work and your colleague says her mother-in-law died over the weekend.

2. Kathleen, a service user, tells you that her grandson has died of a drug overdose. She talks about the police saying he was a drug dealer, but she will not accept this.

3. Anna looked after her sister, Ruth, ever since she got Alzheimer's disease. Ruth attended your day centre 5 days a week. A few days ago Ruth drowned in the canal one evening; she had been wandering and fell in. Today you are going to visit Anna at home because she asked you and a colleague to visit.

4. Cameron and Jock have always sat together at day centre, where they have come for many years. Jock got very ill a few months ago and stopped coming to the centre when he knew he was terminally ill. He died last week; Cameron was at his bedside. This is the first time you have seen Cameron since the death.

5. A new service user, Peter, is very open with staff and other service users about being gay. He tells you his partner, Alec, died of AIDS two months ago.

KEY THINGS TO FIND OUT WHEN WORKING WITH A DYING SERVICE USER

- Where to die?

- Visitors – who to see/not see?

- Information sharing – who should be kept informed? Should any information be withheld?

- Special comforts – to have certain music playing; to be read to etc.

- Who should be there at the end?

- Funeral arrangements

STAGES IN FACING DEATH

1. **Denial and isolation**
   (usually occurs after a person is told they are terminally ill)

2. **Anger**
   (replaces denial and will be vented at random – towards doctors, family, care staff, other service users)

3. **Bargaining**
   (person tries to make an agreement in order to get more time)

4. **Depression**
   (person is no longer in denial or angry but will feel a great sense of loss)

5. **Acceptance**
   (the anger and struggle to accept the inevitable have gone)

THE NEED TO TALK

A dying person may need to talk about:

- Past life

- Regrets

- Secrets

- Unresolved issues

- How they can put certain things right

- Feelings

- Fears

- Hopes

- Dying

- The end

- After death

- The funeral

IMMEDIATELY AFTER DEATH

Immediately after the death, care workers should think about:

- Informing necessary people e.g. GP (to certify death), relatives, friends etc.

- Giving relatives/friends enough time with the body – not rushing them

- Attending the body (this may need to be done by the family/religious members)

- Making arrangements for the body to be moved (contacting funeral director)

- Whether a funeral has to take place within certain time limits (for particular religions)

- Whether a period of mourning is required

STAGES IN GRIEF

1. **Shock and disbelief**
   (the person may say they feel numb; they are failing to accept the loss)

2. **Expressions of grief**
   (shows acute anxiety, pines for the dead person, remembers the good times)

3. **Depression and apathy**
   (becomes irritable, feels despair, a sense of hopelessness and disorganisation)

4. **Signs of recovery**
   (reorganises life)

Chapter 12

Abuse

When the word 'abuse' is used people tend to immediately think of child abuse – very rarely does one immediately think about an older person being the victim of abuse. People also tend to think in terms of physical abuse and sexual abuse rather than the wider forms of abuse and neglect. All care workers need to raise their awareness about abuse and neglect because at some point in their careers they are probably going to come across such a situation. Abuse can happen both in an institution and in the community; a care worker working in a home might discover abuse because:

- abuse is happening within the home

- a service user who is coming in for respite care is being abused in the community

- a service user may disclose that they have been abused in the past.

Day care workers are working with people who live in the community; they might suspect that someone is being abused or a service user might disclose it to them. This chapter will focus on:

- what abuse is

- how to recognise it

- what to do if you suspect or find abuse.

History

The abuse of older people is not a new phenomenon – it has been recognised for a long time (Baker 1975; Burston 1975 and 1977). However, it has not always been given the high profile it deserves because of the ageism which exists in our society; older people are not as emotive as children and are not treated with the same respect as elders in some other cultures and societies.

In the 1980s Mervyn Eastman wrote about older people who were abused by their carers and defined abuse as:

The systematic maltreatment, physical, emotional, or financial, of an elderly person…this may take the form of physical assault, threatening behaviour, neglect and abandonment or sexual assault. (Eastman 1984, p.3)

In 1993 the Department of Health broadened the definition:

Abuse may be described as physical, sexual, psychological, or financial. It may be intentional or unintentional, or the result of neglect. It causes harm to the older person, either temporarily or over a period of time. (DH 1993, p.3)

This development was important because it gave recognition to the fact that neglect and sexual abuse were prevalent (and should be recognised as such – not just included in physical abuse as previously) but also emphasised the fact that abuse could be unintentional.

Case Example

Vicky was 18 years old and had been working in the residential home for a month. She had received no formal training, but was told to 'shadow' Una, who had been working there for 20 years and 'knew everything'. Vicky rough-handled the service users because she had never been shown how to move service users correctly; many of them started getting bruised. Vicky was harming the service users, but it was unintentional.

A major development took place in March 2000 when John Hutton, Minister of Health, launched *No Secrets: Guidance on Developing and Implementing Multi-Agency Policies and Procedures to Protect Vulnerable Adults from Abuse* (DH 2000a). 'Directors of Social Services will be expected to ensure that the local agency codes of practice are developed and implemented by 31st October 2001' (DH 2000b, p.2). Abuse was then defined as: '…a violation of an individual's human and civil rights by any other person or persons' (DH 2000a, p.9). The guidance then went on to say:

> Abuse may consist of a single act or repeated acts. It may be physical, verbal or psychological, it may be an act of neglect or an omission to act, or it may occur when a vulnerable person is persuaded to enter into a financial or sexual transaction to which he or she has not consented, or cannot consent. Abuse can occur in any relationship and may result in significant harm to, or exploitation of, the person subjected to it.

(Department of Health 2000)

Six categories of abuse were given:

- physical

- sexual

- emotional/psychological

- financial/material

- neglect/acts of omission

- discriminatory.

Handout 12.1, p.356

It is always difficult to define abuse and workers can argue that there are 'too many grey areas'. Therefore, in any training session adequate time needs to be allocated to allow workers to talk about what abuse means to them and for them to know how abuse is defined in national as well as local guidance. Handouts 12.1 to 12.4 can be used in training sessions in conjunction with exercises (see Pritchard 1996) which encourage discussion about what constitutes abuse. Participative training is better than bombarding workers with a lot of information in a short space of time. Exercise 12.1 can be used as an introductory exercise early on in a basic awareness course.

It is important that all homes and day centres should have a copy of their local adult abuse policy, which will be available from the social services department. Some homes will have developed their own policies and procedures as well, so care workers need to be familiar with all these documents. Other useful guidance comes from the Nursing and Midwifery Council, which was formerly known as United Kingdom Central Council for Nursing, Midwifery and Health Visiting (UKCC) (UKCC 1999).

Terminology

Terminology regarding the abuse of older people has changed during the past 30 years: 'granny-battering', 'old age abuse', 'elder abuse', 'adult abuse', 'adult protection'. The term **vulnerable adult** is also used frequently in relation to this subject area, defined as a person

> who is or may be in need of community care services by reason of mental or other disability, age or illness; and who is or may be unable to take care of him or herself, or unable to protect him or herself against significant harm or exploitation. (Lord Chancellor's Department 1997, p.68)

Key Questions

Is the service user being harmed in any way
(physical or emotional)?

Is the service user being exploited in any way
(financial or sexual)?

It is important to remember that a person can be harmed physically and emotionally, and that exploitation can be financial or sexual.

The following definition of **significant harm** can also be a useful starting point when thinking about whether a service user is a victim of abuse:

> ...not only ill treatment (including sexual abuse and forms of ill treatment which are not physical), but also the impairment of, or an avoidable deterioration in, physical or mental health; and the impairment of physical, intellectual, emotional, social or behavioural development.

(Lord Chancellor's Department 1997, p.68)

An issue which needs to be discussed at length with care workers is bad practice and abuse. The extreme cases of abuse can be defined and identified more easily than cases where there are more subtle forms of abuse. One should never compare types of abuse, for example, by saying one is more important than another. Any form of abuse is unacceptable and a care worker should be considering how the service user views the abusive act.

Care workers can sometimes view actions as 'just bad practice' and not define them as abuse. It is useful for a trainer to show the opening shots of the video **Abuse in the Care Home** and ask workers whether they think what they see are forms of abuse, before showing the rest of the video. Quiz Sheet 12.1 can also be used to facilitate discussion.

Handouts 12.3 and 12.4, pp.358–9

Institutional abuse

An institution is somewhere which has rules and regulations; we have all been in one at some time in our lives (e.g. school, hospital). Exercise 12.2 will help care workers to think about what has happened to them when they have been in an institution and how they behaved. It is important to think whether a service user who comes into a home or day centre might react in the same way. The word 'institution' conjures up all sorts of images. Many older people might think of the old workhouse; others of us will have different images. The exercise will help care workers to think about their own experiences.

As we have seen earlier in the manual people can sometimes get confused by the meaning of words. Exercise 12.3 looks at meanings of words connected to an institution.

Having completed Exercises 12.2 and 12.3 the trainer should discuss the definition of institutional abuse from *No Secrets* using Handout 12.7.

> Neglect and poor professional practice also need to be taken into account. This may take the form of isolated incidents of poor or unsatisfactory professional practice, at one end of the spectrum, through to pervasive ill treatment or gross misconduct at the other. Repeated instances of poor care may be an indication of more serious problems and this is sometimes referred to as **institutional abuse**. (DH 2000a, p.10)

Care workers need to realise that they themselves can become institutionalised when working in a home or day centre and they constantly need to review their own practices. It is also important to recognise that institutional abuse is not just about staff abusing service users; it must be remembered that:

- a care worker can abuse a service user
- a service user can abuse a care worker
- a service user can abuse a service user
- an outsider can abuse a service user
- a manager/colleague can abuse a care worker.

Handout 12.8, p.363

What have you seen?

People new to social care may never have thought much about abuse and may be shocked or upset when having to be trained on such an emotive topic. More experienced workers may be hardened to the fact that abuse goes on because of what they have seen in previous places of work. It is important for care workers to understand that abuse *does* happen. A useful exercise is to show the video **Abuse in the Care Home** and get care workers to write down what they have seen in their own experience. Alternatively, Exercise 12.4 can be used. A trainer should be prepared for responses such as: 'That's normal in a nursing home'; 'It's gone on for years, you can't do anything about it'; 'I reported what I saw. Nothing was done, so I left.' A trainer must keep emphasising the fact that abuse *must* be reported and that steps can be taken to stop it.

Why abuse happens

It has already been said that when care workers are first learning about abuse it is important not to bombard them with too much information because they will not take it all in. Abuse is a very complex issue and there are many causal factors which can contribute to an abusive situation. A trainer should emphasise that adult abuse is not just about carers' stress. There should be some discussion around possible root causes of abuse in homes or day centres:

- lack of education/training
- staff groups/factions
- the manager
- existing regimes
- the environment
- low staff morale
- low staffing levels
- the characteristics of staff
- the characteristics of service users.

Handouts 12.9 and 12.10 can be used to facilitate discussion.

Recognising abuse

The difficulty in recognising abuse should never be underestimated. Most of us have 'gut-feelings' at some time or other and would probably say that those feelings have usually been right. It is good to verbalise what you feel, but gathering actual evidence is what is needed.

It takes time to learn the signs and symptoms of abuse. No one can expect a care worker to attend a basic awareness course on abuse and 'know it all'. It is necessary to develop an understanding of why abuse might happen (and there are many different theories about this) as well as learning the indicators. A further difficulty is that many signs and symptoms of abuse could be indicators of other conditions. Therefore, it is imperative that care workers are also trained not to jump to conclusions, but to keep an open mind while monitoring situations.

In the past a lot has been written about carers' stress causing abusive situations. This does happen, but there can be many other root causes of abuse. It is important that care workers do not fall into the trap of stereotyping people; that is, that the typical victim is female and the typical abuser is male. Anyone could be a victim or an abuser.

Good Practice Points

It is wrong to stereotype.

Anyone could be a victim or an abuser.

Case Examples

- Harold attended day centre once a week. He often presented with bruises and cuts. He eventually disclosed that his wife battered him and had done so throughout their marriage.

- Eddie was a male care worker who regularly had sexual intercourse with female service users with dementia. When police investigated they found that he had a criminal record for sex offences.

- Jane had worked as a volunteer and advocate for many years. She liked to visit older people in care homes, from whom she took money.

- William was 79 years old when he was raped by his male carer.

- Anita worked in the day centre and regularly bullied both her colleagues and service users.

- Ethel regularly swore at staff in the day centre and threw things at them.

It is also important to acknowledge that vulnerable people can often be targeted and groomed by an abuser.

Case Example

Millicent was 67 years old and had moderate learning disabilities. After her mother died she was befriended by Jack, whom she had met in the local café where she had her breakfast each morning. After knowing Jack a year, Millicent no longer had control over her finances. He cashed her pension and he had persuaded Millicent to put her bank account into joint names with him as co-signatory. When he started having sexual inter-course with her, Millicent told day care workers that 'she was being hurt inside'.

Information regarding indicators can be found in Handouts 12.11, 12.12, 12.13 and 12.14, but trainers should refer to Pritchard (1996 and 2001a) for detailed exercises and case studies in order to further develop care workers' understanding.

It is important to stress to care workers that abuse often remains well hidden either because the victim wants to maintain the relationship with the abuser, especially if it is a family member, or because s/he is scared to speak out because of the possible re-percussions. Abuse is hard to detect and care workers can have a crucial role in identi-fying abuse by monitoring changes in behaviour. Handout 12.15 is particularly important; care workers need to understand that changes in behaviour can occur over long periods of time (months and years) and may not be immediate. It can be helpful to show the case study of Annie in the video **Abuse in the Care Home** to illustrate this point.

What to do

A care worker could find themselves in many situations where they might have to deal with abuse – some of which may or may not be straightforward:

- Care worker sees a definite abusive act.

- Service user discloses that s/he is a victim of abuse.

- An abuser (this could be a colleague or family member) tells you they have abused a service user.

- Care worker picks up signs of abuse over a period of time but service user denies abuse is going on.

- Care worker has a 'gut feeling' that a service user is being abused.

- Care worker is concerned about what is going on in the workplace (e.g. current practices, lack of facilities etc.).

In any of these situations a care worker must report to their line manager and if no action is taken then it must be reported to someone higher up in the organisation. No one feels comfortable reporting suspected abuse, however, a care worker must:

- check policy procedures

- report to line manager

- record.

There are other people who can help:

- social services – there might be an Adult Protection Co-ordinator in post.

- police

- National Care Standards Commission

- trade union

- personnel department.

Handout 12.16, p.371

A care worker must always write down what they have seen or heard and record who they reported to and at what time they did this.

A care worker should also find out whether a whistleblowing policy exists within the organisation in addition to the adult abuse policy, disciplinary procedure and complaints procedure.

None of us really knows how we would react if we found ourselves in certain situations. We can anticipate what we might do, but we can never be certain. Sometimes we are so shocked by something we can become verbally paralysed. Training sessions should introduce situations which could occur so that care workers can discuss how they *should* react; that is, they need to anticipate what they would actually *say* and *do*. Care workers should be made aware that they should always try not to contaminate the evidence; that is, if any questions have to be asked, they should use open questions rather than leading questions. A useful technique is reflection; that is, the exact words are repeated back to the person but inflection is put in the voice to make it a question (refer back to Chapter 7).

Case Example

Service user discloses: 'That care worker, Debbie, hit me hard yesterday.'

Care worker uses **leading questions**:

'Did she hit you with her hand or with something else?'

'Did she hit you on the face?'

Better responses would have been:

'Do you want to tell me what happened?'

'Debbie hit you hard?' (**reflection technique**)

Exercise 12.5 and Handout 12.17 are designed to help care workers think about good practice in saying and doing.

Suggested reading

Action on Elder Abuse (April 2002) *Responding to Abuse in Residential and Day Care Settings* leaflet. London: AEA.

Department of Health (1993) *No Longer Afraid: The Safeguard of Older People in Domestic Settings.* London: HMSO.

Department of Health (2000a) *No Secrets: Guidance on Developing and Implementing Multi-Agency Policies and Procedures to Protect Vulnerable Adults from Abuse.* London: HMSO.

Pritchard, J. (1996) *Working with Elder Abuse: A Training Manual for Home Care, Residential and Day Care Staff.* London: Jessica Kingsley Publishers.

Pritchard, J. (2000) *The Needs of Older Women: Services for Victims of Elder Abuse and Other Abuse.* Bristol: The Policy Press.

Pritchard, J. (2001a) *Becoming a Trainer in Adult Abuse Work.* London: Jessica Kingsley Publishers.

Pritchard, J. (ed) (2001b) *Good Practice with Vulnerable Adults.* London: Jessica Kingsley Publishers.

Pritchard, J. (2001c) *Male Victims of Elder Abuse: Their Experiences and Needs.* London: Jessica Kingsley Publishers.

Useful organisations

Action on Elder Abuse

Astral House, 1268 London Road, London SW16 4ER

Tel: 020 8765 7000 Fax: 020 8679 4074

E-mail: aea@ace.org.uk Website: www.elderabuse.org.uk

Ann Craft Trust (ACT)

Centre for Social Work, University Park, Nottingham NG7 2RD

Tel: 0115 951 5400

Website: www.nottingham.ac.uk/sociology/act/

National Care Standards Commission

St Nicholas' Building, St Nicholas' Street, Newcastle NE1 1RF

Tel: 0191 233 3535 Fax: 0191 233 3569

E-mail: enquiries@ncsc.gsi.gov.uk Website: www.carestandards.org.uk

POPAN (The Prevention of Professional Abuse Network)

1 Wyvil Court, Wyvil Road, London SW8 2TG

Tel: 020 7622 6334 Fax: 020 7622 9788

E-mail: info@POPAN.org.uk Website: www.popan.org.uk

Voice UK

Room B11, The College Business Centre, Uttoxeter New Road, Derby DE22 3WZ

Tel: 01332 869311/2/4 Fax: 01332 869318 Helpline: 0870 013 3965

E-mail: voiceuk@clara.net Website: www.voiceuk.clara.net

📼 VIDEO

Abuse in the Care Home

WHAT IS ABUSE?

Objective

To get care workers to think about what abuse means to them.

Participants

Small groups.

Time

10 minutes.

Equipment

Flipchart paper and pens.
Copies of Handouts 12.1, 12.2, 12.3, 12.4.

Task

1. Having been given Handout 12.1, participants are asked to discuss what types of abuse might be put under each category.

2. Groups are asked to write 3 examples of abuse under each category on the flipchart paper.

Feedback

1. Trainer goes through each category of abuse and asks for feedback from each group.

2. Trainer gives out Handouts 12.2 to 12.4.

3. Large group discussion focusing on definitions.

BEING IN AN INSTITUTION

Objective

To get care workers to compare their own experiences of being in an institution to those of a service user in a care home or day centre.

Participants

Work individually; then to share with one other person.

Time

5–10 minutes to complete the Responding to Institutionalisation Questionnaire (Handout 12.5); 10 minute discussion in pairs.

Equipment

Trainer to photocopy Handout 12.5.

Task

1. Participants are asked to complete the questionnaire on Handout 12.5.

2. They share the questionnaire with one other person in the group.

Feedback

1. Discussion in large group. Trainer facilitates discussion by asking whether participants had conformed or rebelled. Those who rebelled should be asked what they did and why.

2. Trainer then brings discussion round to focus on service users, i.e. will they conform or rebel; how will they do this; how can they be empowered by care workers?

Note for trainer

This exercise can have two purposes. It can be used to look at how everyone can become institutionalised at some point in their life when working on institutional abuse, but it can also be used to look at needs in relation to leisure, education, interests and what is currently offered in homes and day centres.

WORDS AND INSTITUTIONS

Objective

To ensure that care workers understand the meaning of 'institution', 'institutional', 'institutionalise'.

Participants

Small groups.

Time

15 minutes.

Equipment

Flipchart paper and pens.
Copies of Handout 12.6.

Task

1. Pretend you are going to write a dictionary. You are required to write definitions for the following words:

    (a) institution

    (b) institutional

    (c) institutionalise.

2. In your group discuss possible meanings and definitions.

3. Write the three definitions on the flipchart paper.

Feedback

1. The trainer asks each group to present their definitions, taking one word at a time.

2. At the end of the feedback, the trainer gives out Handout 12.6 and full discussion follows.

WHAT HAVE YOU SEEN?

Objective

For care workers to share their experiences.

Participants

Work individually; then share in small groups.

Time

10 minutes for individual work; 15 minutes in small groups.

Equipment

Paper and pens.

Task

1. Write down what you have seen when working in a care home or day centre, which you would now consider to be a form of abuse.

2. Talk about your experiences with two or three other people in the group.

Feedback

1. Groups will feed back the types of abuse they have seen.

2. Trainer will invite discussion about what was done at the time and whether such situations would be dealt with differently now.

Note for trainer

During this exercise some participants may start to feel guilty because they realise that they have done something in the past which may be considered to be abuse or they may disclose something that is going on in their current workplace. The trainer needs to be extremely sensitive to these matters and allow time for the workers to talk about their feelings. However, ground rules should have been set at the beginning of any formal training course explaining that the trainer may have to break confidentiality if abuse is disclosed (see *Becoming a Trainer in Adult Abuse Work*, Pritchard 2001, pp.60–62).

SAYING AND DOING

Objective

To make care workers think about what they would say immediately when they found themselves in a situation and then what they would do.

Participants

Small groups.

Equipment

Handout 12.17 to be photocopied by trainer.
Flipchart paper and pens.

Time

30 minutes.

Task

1. Discuss each scenario in turn.

2. Make a list of things you would say, i.e. either comments or questions. Write the actual words you would use. It does not matter how many responses you put down – participants may have a variety of ideas.

3. Write down what you would do next.

Feedback

1. Each group presents their answers.

2. Full discussion about issues raised.

QUIZ SHEET 12.1

WHAT IS IT?

1. Hannah has dementia and likes to wander around the care home. Care worker says she has to sit in the lounge.

    Abuse/Bad practice/Don't know

2. Ellen weighs sixteen stone. She is not allowed to have puddings. She is given fruit.

    Abuse/Bad practice/Don't know

3. Service user calls another service user 'Stupid cow'.

    Abuse/Bad practice/Don't know

4. Care worker tells Mr Patel: 'We're short staffed and cannot take you to the mosque.'

    Abuse/Bad practice/Don't know

5. Marion works extra shifts to boost her low income. This means sometimes working an early shift, having a few hours off and then returning for the night shift. She has started falling asleep on duty.

    Abuse/Bad practice/Don't know

6. A Jewish man is given pork to eat. It is not considered to be important to follow his religious beliefs because he is confused.

    Abuse/Bad practice/Don't know

7. A gay service user is not allowed to have his partner in his bedroom when he visits.

    Abuse/Bad practice/Don't know

8. Two male service users like to play cards into the early hours of the morning. Night staff tell them they have to be in bed by 11.00p.m.

    Abuse/Bad practice/Don't know

9. A manager tells service users they cannot have newspapers delivered to the home.

    Abuse/Bad practice/Don't know

10. Simon is 70 years old and has paranoid schizophrenia and lives with his parents who are in their 90s. His parents manage his money and now he has stopped attending the day centre because they say he cannot afford it.

    Abuse/Bad practice/Don't know

11. Sharon is a day care worker who often pops out to the supermarket for service users. She always goes to Tesco's and uses her own reward card.

    Abuse/Bad practice/Don't know

12. Ivy likes to touch Danny, who is a day centre worker, on his bottom. He does not say anything.

    Abuse/Bad practice/Don't know

13. Desmond has epilepsy. He is told he cannot go on the annual day care outing because he had a fit last year and 'it's too risky'.

    Abuse/Bad practice/Don't know

14. A care worker tells Annie she cannot play bingo because she's 'been a bad girl' as she wet the chair before lunch.

    Abuse/Bad practice/Don't know

15. Two care workers stand in front of a service user
and talk about another service user.

                                Abuse/Bad practice/Don't know

16. An Asian woman is bathed by a male care worker.

                                Abuse/Bad practice/Don't know

17. Manager tells a care worker in the staff room where
other colleagues are having a break: 'You've really
made a mess of Hettie's review form.'

                                Abuse/Bad practice/Don't know

18. Care worker says to service user: 'Come on sweetheart,
it's time for dinner.'   Abuse/Bad practice/Don't know

19. A service user has complained that she is not getting
enough to eat. Care staff do not do anything when she
says this.   Abuse/Bad practice/Don't know

20. Service user asks if he can have a bath when he attends
day centre. Care workers say they have not got enough
time to provide this service.

                                Abuse/Bad practice/Don't know

21. Sid likes to have three tots of whisky during the course of
the evening; he has done this throughout his adult life. The
night staff say that he is consuming too much alcohol.

                                Abuse/Bad practice/Don't know

CATEGORIES OF ADULT ABUSE

- Physical

- Sexual

- Emotional/
psychological

- Financial/material

- Neglect/acts of omission

- Discriminatory

FORMS OF ABUSE

The Department of Health has said a consensus has emerged identifying the following main different forms of abuse:

- **Physical abuse** – including hitting, slapping, pushing, kicking, misuse of medication, restraint, or inappropriate sanctions.

- **Sexual abuse** – including rape and sexual assault or sexual acts to which the vulnerable adult has not consented, or could not consent or was pressured into consenting.

- **Psychological abuse** – including emotional abuse, threats of harm or abandonment, deprivation of contact, humiliation, blaming, controlling, intimidation, coercion, harassment, verbal abuse, isolation or withdrawal from services or supportive networks.

- **Financial or material abuse** – including theft, fraud, exploitation, pressure in connection with wills, property or inheritance or financial transactions, or the misuse or misappropriation of property, possessions or benefits.

- **Neglect and acts of omission** – including ignoring medical or physical care needs, failure to provide access to appropriate health, social care or educational services, the withholding of the necessities of life, such as medication, adequate nutrition and heating.

- **Discriminatory abuse** – including racist, sexist, that based on a person's disability, and other forms of harassment, slurs or similar treatment.

(From: Section 2.7 Department of Health (2000) *No Secrets*. London: HMSO.)

KEY DEFINITIONS FROM *NO SECRETS*

A vulnerable adult is a person:

who is or may be in need of community care services by reason of mental or other disability, age or illness; and who is or may be unable to take care of him or herself, or unable to protect him or herself against significant harm or exploitation.

(From: Lord Chancellor's Department (1997) *Who Decides?*
London: The Stationery Office.)

Abuse is:

a violation of an individual's human and civil rights by any other person or persons.

(From: page 9, Department of Health (2000) *No Secrets.*
London: HMSO.)

Forms of abuse:

- Physical abuse

- Sexual abuse

- Psychological abuse

- Financial or material

- Neglect and acts of omission

- Discriminatory abuse

(From: Department of Health (2000) *No Secrets.* London: HMSO.)

NATIONAL DEFINITIONS

Abuse:

The systematic maltreatment, physical, emotional or financial, of an elderly person...this may take the form of physical assault, threatening behaviour, neglect, abandonment or sexual assault.

(From: page 3, Eastman, M. (1984) *Old Age Abuse*. London: Age Concern.)

Abuse may be described as physical, sexual, psychological or financial. It may be intentional or unintentional, or the result of neglect. It causes harm to the older person, either temporarily or over a period of time.

(From: page 3, Department of Health (1993) *No Longer Afraid: The Safeguard of Older People in Domestic Settings*. London: HMSO.)

Elder abuse is a single or repeated act or lack of appropriate action occurring within any relationship where there is an expectation of trust which causes harm or distress to an older person.

(From: Action on Elder Abuse (1995) *Bulletin No 11* London: AEA.)

...a violation of an individual's human and civil rights by any other person or persons.

(From: page 9, Department of Health (2000) *No Secrets*. London: HMSO.)

Abuse may consist of a single act or repeated acts. It may be physical, verbal or psychological, it may be an act of neglect or an omission to act, or it may occur when a vulnerable person is persuaded to enter into a financial or sexual transaction to which he or she has not consented, or cannot consent. Abuse can occur in any relationship and may result in significant harm to, or exploitation of, the person subjected to it.

(From: page 9, Department of Health (2000) *No Secrets*. London: HMSO.)

Significant harm:

...not only ill treatment (including sexual abuse and forms of ill treatment which are not physical), but also the impairment of, or an avoidable deterioration in, physical or mental health; and the impairment of physical, intellectual, emotional, social or behavioural development.

(From: page 68, Lord Chancellor's Department (1997) *Who Decides?*: London: The Stationery Office.)

RESPONDING TO INSTITUTIONALISATION QUESTIONNAIRE

Age:

Gender:

List institutions you have been in during your lifetime:

Was your behaviour regimented in any way in these institutions? If so, how?

Did you conform or did you rebel?

At this point in your life what are your main interests and hobbies (be sure to list any unusual ones)?

Are they different to 10 years ago?

Think of one adult family member or friend who is in a different age group to you (at least 10 years' difference). What are his/her interests and hobbies (again be sure to list any unusual ones)?

SOME MEANINGS OF WORDS

Institution:

1. An important organisation or public body, such as a university, bank, hospital or church.

2. An organisation providing residential care for people with special needs.

3. An established law or custom.

4. A well-established and familiar person or thing.

5. The action of instituting.

Institutional:

1. Of, in, or like an institution.

2. Typical of an institution, especially in being regimented or unimaginative.

Institutionalise:

1. Establish as a norm in an organisation or culture.

2. Place in a residential institution.

3. Suffer the adverse effects of long-term residence in a residential institution.

(From: *Oxford Compact English Dictionary* (2000))

INSTITUTIONAL ABUSE

Neglect and poor professional practice also need to be taken into account. This may take the form of isolated incidents of poor or unsatisfactory professional practice, at one end of the spectrum, through to pervasive ill treatment or gross misconduct at the other. Repeated instances of poor care may be an indication of more serious problems and this is sometimes referred to as **institutional abuse**.

(From: Section 2.9, Department of Health (2000) *No Secrets*. London: HMSO.)

WHO CAN ABUSE IN A HOME OR DAY CENTRE

- A care worker can abuse a service user

- A service user can abuse a care worker

- A service user can abuse a service user

- An outsider can abuse a service user

- A manager/colleague can abuse a care worker

POSSIBLE CAUSES OF ABUSE IN HOMES AND DAY CENTRES

- Lack of education/training

- Staff groups/factions

- The manager

- Existing regimes

- The environment

- Low staff morale

- Low staffing levels

- The characteristics of staff

- The characteristics of service users

GOOD PRACTICE TIPS: CHECKLIST

Cause for concern

Staffing: inadequate recruitment/selection practice; inadequate or no induction; inadequate practice guidance and standards; poor or no support, supervision, appraisal or development; poor or no training; poor pay and conditions; undervaluing of staff; staff working alone or on a one to one basis; working under pressure; authoritarian or laissez-faire regime; high level of sickness; high level of turnover; inappropriate alcohol consumption by staff.

Practice: failure to develop clear philosophy/purpose/aim; senior staff being in post a long time thus having a high level of authority and perhaps entrenched views; under resourcing – staff, equipment, provisions; dull or depressing lifestyle for users; poor medical/nursing/personal care; few outside contacts; no advocacy scheme or complaints procedures; poor recording; poor administration; no internal audit/evaluation; a lack of openness about practice or procedure – an air of secrecy; fixed times of rising and going to bed; bathing and toilet routines not geared to the individual.

Environment: poor physical conditions; overcrowding; lack of equipment or damaged equipment; neglected furniture and fittings; overly clean; inadequately clean.

Individual staff: lack of interest and commitment; lack of knowledge, understanding or concern for the residents; personal problems including health problems; inability to relate to a particular resident.

External contact: pattern of incidents of concern; high level of complaints but none proven; difficulties or delays in access to people and premises; over controlling regime; strict visiting times.

(From: Hughes, A. (2001) 'The Role of the Registration and Inspection Officer.' In J. Pritchard (ed) *Good Practice with Vulnerable Adults*. London: Jessica Kingsley Publishers.)

PHYSICAL INDICATIONS OF ABUSE
(THIS INCLUDES PHYSICAL NEGLECT)

- Multiple bruising, not consistent with a fall

- Black eyes, slap marks, kick marks, other bruises

- Burns, not consistent with scorching by direct heat

- Fractures not consistent with falls

- Stench of urine or faeces

- Indications of malnutrition or overfeeding

- Absence of mobility aids

- Administration of inappropriate drugs or the absence of necessary medication

INDICATORS OF SEXUAL ABUSE

- Genital or urinary irritation

- Frequent infections (evidence of vaginal discharge may be found on knickers)

- Bleeding (blood can be found on underwear, nightclothes)

- Sexually transmitted disease

- Bruising on inner thighs

- Difficulty in walking/sitting

- Sudden onset of confusion

- Depression

- Nightmares

- Severe upset or agitation when the older person is being bathed, dressed, undressed, or medically examined (or when these things are suggested)

- Conversation regularly becomes of a sexual nature

INDICATORS OF EMOTIONAL ABUSE (THIS INCLUDES EMOTIONAL NEGLECT)

- Insomnia/deprivation of sleep or need for excessive sleep

- Change in appetite

- Unusual weight gain/loss

- Weepiness/unusual bouts of sobbing/crying

- Unexplained paranoia

- Low self-esteem

- Excessive fear/anxiety

- Ambivalence

INDICATORS OF FINANCIAL ABUSE

- Unexplained or sudden inability to pay bills (e.g. rent, gas, electricity, no money for food/shopping)

- Unexplained or sudden withdrawal of money from post office/bank/building society accounts

- Disparity between assets and living conditions

- Lack of receptivity by the older person or relative/neighbour to any necessary assistance requiring expenditure, when finances are not a problem

- Extraordinary interest by family members or other people in the older person's assets/will

KNOWN REACTIONS TO ABUSE

- The denial (often forthright) that anything is amiss, with an accompanying emphasis that things 'have never been better'

- Resignation, stoicism, and, sometimes, an acceptance of incidents as being part of being old/vulnerable

- Withdrawal from activity, communication and participation

- Marked change in behaviour and inappropriate attachments. Fear, subsequently combined with depression and a sense of hopelessness

- Mental confusion

- Anger and physical/verbal outbursts

- Seeking attention/protection, often from numerous sources (some of which can be unlikely)

WHAT TO DO WHEN YOU FIND OR SUSPECT ABUSE

What To Do

- Check policy and procedures

- Report to line manager

- Record

Who Can Help

- Social services (e.g. Adult Protection Co-ordinator)

- Police

- National Care Standards Commission

- Trade Union

- Personnel Department

SAYING AND DOING

1. Every night a gang of teenagers shouts 'wrinklies' and 'coffin dodgers' outside the care home.

2. You suspect that a colleague is drinking on duty and you are worried that it is affecting her care of service users.

3. A female service user tells a day centre worker that the male home carer has touched her breasts.

4. You see a colleague walk into a service user's bedroom without knocking.

5. You overhear a service user say to a black service user: 'I hate wogs like you.'

6. Charles visits his sister Edwina, who has dementia, every week in her nursing home. One day a care worker goes into Edwina's bedroom when she hears shouts for help. She finds Edwina and Charles in bed together.

7. You are bathing Mr Richards who comes in for regular respite care. You see three cigarette burns on his lower back.

8. You take a group of service users (some of whom are confused) to the pub for lunch. The landlord says: 'I know you're from up the road. We don't want the likes of them in here.'

9. Service user says she wants to die. She refuses to eat or drink.

10. A colleague tells you that she has lost her temper with a service user. She has hit the service user and sworn at her.

BVS Videos

This training manual can be used in conjunction with a series of videos produced by BVS Ltd. Each video comes with a CD-Rom containing instructor guide, questionnaires, answer sheets and staff training records. The relevant videos are:

Abuse in the Care Home

Death, Dying and Bereavement

Effective Communication 1

Effective Communication 2 (Written)

Emergency First Aid

Fire Drills and Evacuation

Fire Prevention

Food Hygiene

Health and Safety

Managing Challenging Behaviour

Moving and Handling

Needs of the Service User

Principles of Care

Risk Assessment (Health and Safety)

Risk Assessment (Moving and Handling)

Role of the Care Worker

Supervision

Contact details for BVS Ltd:

BVS
London House
271–273 King Street
Hammersmith
London W6 9LZ
Tel: 020 8233 2913
Fax: 020 8233 2914
E-mail: info@bvs-uk.com
Website: www.bvs-uk.com

Useful Organisations: Contact Details

Action on Elder Abuse

Astral House, 1268 London Road, London SW16 4ER

Tel: 020 8765 7000 Fax: 020 8679 4074 Helpline: 0808 808 8141

E-mail: aea@ace.org.uk Website: www.elderabuse.org.uk

Age Concern England

Astral House, 1268 London Road, London SW16 4ER

Tel: 020 8765 7200 Fax: 020 8765 7211

E-mail: ace@ace.org.uk Website: www.ageconcern.org.uk

Alcohol Concern

Waterbridge House, 32–36 Loman Street, London SE1 0EE

Tel: 020 7928 7377 Fax: 020 7928 4644

E-mail: contact@alcoholconcern.org.uk Website: www.alcoholconcern.org.uk

Alzheimer's Society

Gordon House, 10 Greencoat Place, London SW1P 1PH

Tel: 020 7306 0606 Fax: 020 7306 0808

E-mail: info@alzheimers.org.uk Website: www.alzheimers.org.uk

Ann Craft Trust (ACT)

Centre for Social Work, University Park, Nottingham NG7 2RD

Tel: 0115 951 5400

Website: www.nottingham.ac.uk/sociology/act/

Arthritis Care

18 Stephenson Way, London NW1 2HD

Tel: 020 7380 6500 Fax: 020 7380 6505

Website: arthritiscare.org.uk

Association for Residential Care (ARC)

Arc House, Marsden Street, Chesterfield, Derbyshire, S40 1JY

Tel: 01246 555043 Fax: 01246 555045

E-mail: contact.us@arcuk.org.uk Website: www.arcuk.org.uk

British Colostomy Association

15 Station Road, Reading, Berkshire, RG1 1LG

Tel: 0118 939 1537 Fax: 0118 956 9095

E-mail: sue@bcass.org.uk Website: www.bcass.org.uk

British Dyslexia Association

98 London Road, Reading RG1 5AU

Tel: 0118 966 2677 Fax: 0118 935 1927 Helpline: 0118 966 8271

E-mail (Helpline): info@dyslexiahelp-bda.demon.co.uk

(Admin): admin@bda-dyslexia.demon.co.uk Website: www.bda-dyslexia.org.uk

British Epilepsy Association (Epilepsy Action)

New Anstey House, Gate Way Drive, Yeadon, Leeds LS19 7XY

Tel: 0113 210 8850 Fax: 0808 800 555 Helpline: 0808 800 5050

E-mail: helpline@epilepsy.org.uk Website: www.epilepsy.org.uk

British Heart Foundation

14 Fitzhardinge Street, London W1H 6DH

Tel: 020 7935 0185 Fax: 020 7486 5820

E-mail: internet@bhf.org.uk Website: www.bhf.org.uk

British Institute of Learning Disabilities (BILD)

Campion House, Green Street, Kidderminster, Worcestershire DY10 3PP

Tel: 01562 723025 Fax: 01562 723029

E-mail: enquiries@bild.org.uk Website: www.bild.org.uk

Carers UK

Ruth Pitter House, 20–25 Glasshouse Yard, London EC1A 4JT

Tel: 020 7490 8818 Fax: 020 7490 8824 Minicom: 020 7251 8969

CarersLine 0808 808 777

E-mail: info@ukcarers.org Website: www.carersonline.org.uk

Centre for Policy on Ageing (CPA)

19–23 Ironmonger Row, London EC1V 3QP

Tel: 020 7553 6500 Fax: 020 7553 6501

E-mail: cpa@cpa.org.uk Website: www.cpa.org.uk

Change (works and campaigns for people with both a learning disability and a sensory impairment)

Block D Hatcham Mews Business Centre, Hatcham Park Mews, London SE14 5QA

Tel: 020 7639 4312 Fax: 020 7639 4317

E-mail: contact@changeuk.demon.co.uk Website: www.changepeople.co.uk

Commission for Racial Equality

St Dunstan's House, 201–211 Borough High Street, London SE1 1GZ

Tel: 020 7939 0000 Fax: 020 7939 0001

E-mail: info@cre.gov.uk Website: www.cre.gov.uk

Continence Foundation

307 Hatton Square, 16 Baldwins Gardens, London EC1N 7RJ

Tel: 020 7404 6875 Fax: 020 7404 6876 Helpline: 0845 345 0165

E-mail: continence.foundation@dial.pipex.com

Website: www.continence-foundation.org.uk

Counsel and Care

Twyman House, 16 Bonny Street, London NW1 9PG

Tel: 020 7241 8555 Fax: 020 7267 6877 Advice: 0845 300 7585

E-mail: advice@counselandcare.org.uk Website: www.counselandcare.org.uk

Cruse Bereavement Care

Cruse House, 126 Sheen Road, Richmond, Surrey TW9 1UR

Tel: 020 8939 9530 Fax: 020 8940 7638 Helpline: 0870 167 1677

E-mail: info@crusebereavementcare.org.uk

Website: www.crusebereavementcare.org.uk

Department of Health

PO Box 777, London SE1 6XH **or**

Richmond House, 79 Whitehall, London SW1A 2NS

Tel: 020 7210 4850

E-mail: dhmail@doh.gsi.gov.uk Website: www.doh.gov.uk

Diabetes UK

10 Parkway, London NW1 7AA

Tel: 020 7424 1000 Fax: 020 7424 1001

E-mail: info@diabetes.org.uk Website: www.diabetes.org.uk

Disabled Living Foundation

380–384 Harrow Road, London W9 2HU

Tel: 020 7289 6111 Fax: 020 7266 2922 Textphone: 020 7432 8009

Helpline: 0845 130 9177

E-mail: dlfinfo@dlf.org.uk Website: www.dlf.org.uk

Hearing Concern

7–11 Armstrong Road, London W3 7JL

Tel: 020 8743 1110 Fax: 020 0742 9043 Helpdesk: 0845 074 4600

E-mail: fiona@hearingconcern.com Website: www.hearingconcern.co.uk

Help the Aged

207–221 Pentonville Road, London N1 9UZ

Tel: 020 7278 1114 Fax: 020 7278 1116 Seniorline: 0808 800 6565

E-mail: info@helptheaged.org.uk Website: www.helptheaged.org.uk

Human Rights Unit Helpdesk

Home Office, 50 Queen Anne's Gate, London SW1H 9AT

Website: www.homeoffice.gov.uk/hract

Huntington's Disease Association

108 Battersea High Street, London SW11 3HP

Tel: 020 7223 7000 Fax: 020 7223 9489

E-mail: info@hda.org.uk Website: www.hda.org.uk

Lord Chancellor's Department

Selborne House, 54–60 Victoria Street, London SW1E 6QW

Tel: 020 7210 8500 Fax: 0207 210 1265

E-mail: general.queries@lcdhq.gsi.gov.uk Website: www.lcd.gov.uk

Macmillan Cancer Relief

89 Albert Embankment, London SE1 7UQ

Tel: 020 7840 7840 Fax: 020 7840 7841 Cancerline: 0808 808 2020

E-mail: cancerline@macmillan.org.uk Website. www.macmillan.org.uk

Marie Curie Cancer Care

89 Albert Embankment, London SE1 7TP

Tel: 020 7599 7777 Fax: 020 7599 7778

E-mail: info@mariecurie.org.uk Website: www.mariecurie.org.uk

MENCAP (Understanding learning disability)

123 Golders Lane, London EC1Y 0RT

Tel: 020 7454 0454 Fax: 020 7696 5540

E-mail: information@mencap.org.uk Website: www.mencap.org.uk

MIND (National Association for Mental Health)

15–19 Broadway, London E15 4BQ

Tel: 020 8519 2122 Fax: 020 8522 1725 Mindinfoline: 0845 766 0163

E-mail: enquiries@mind.org.uk Website: www.mind.org.uk

Multiple Sclerosis Society

MS National Centre, 372 Edgware Road, Staples Corner, London NW2 6ND

Tel: 020 8438 0700 Helpline: 0808 800 8000

Website: www.mssociety.org.uk

Muscular Dystrophy Campaign

7–11 Prescott Place, London SW4 6BS

Tel: 020 7720 8055 Fax: 020 7498 0670 Helpline: 020 7720 8055

E-mail: info@muscular-dystrophy.org Website: www.muscular-dystrophy.org

National Association for Providers of Activities for Older People (NAPA)

5 Tavistock Place, London WC1H 9SN

Tel/Fax: 020 7383 5757

National Association for the Relief of Paget's Disease

Marilyn McCallum, 323 Manchester Road, Walkden, Worsley, Manchester M28 3HH

Tel: 0161 799 4646 Fax: 0161 799 6511

E-mail: director@paget.org.uk Website: www.paget.org.uk

National Care Standards Commission

St Nicholas' Building, St Nicholas' Street, Newcastle NE1 1RF

Tel: 0191 233 3535 Fax: 0191 233 3569

E-mail: enquiries@ncsc.gsi.gov.uk Website: www.carestandards.org.uk

National Schizophrenia Fellowship (NSF)
[Rethink is the operating name of NSF]

28 Castle Street, Kingston Upon Thames, Surrey KT1 1SS

Tel: 020 8547 3937 Fax: 020 8547 3862 Advice Line: 020 8974 6814

E-mail: info@nsf.org.uk Website: www.nsf.org.uk

Nursing and Midwifery Council (formerly UKCC)

23 Portland Place, London W1B 1PZ

Tel: 020 7637 7181 Fax: 020 7436 2924

E-mail: advice@nmc-uk.org Website: www.nmc-uk.org

Parkinson's Disease Society

215 Vauxhall Bridge Road, London SW1V 1EJ

Tel: 020 7931 8080 Fax: 020 7233 9908 Helpline: 0808 800 0303

E-mail: enquiries@parkinsons.org.uk Website: www.parkinsons.org.uk

Peter Honey Learning Publications Limited

10 Linden Avenue, Maidenhead, Berkshire SL6 6HB

Tel: 01628 633946 Fax: 01628 633262

E-mail: info@peterhoney.com Website: www.peterhoneylearning.com

POPAN (The Prevention of Professional Abuse Network)

1 Wyvil Court, Wyvil Road, London SW8 2TG

Tel: 020 7622 6334 Fax: 020 7622 9788

E-mail: info@POPAN.org.uk Website: www.popan.org.uk

RNIB (Royal National Institute of the Blind)

105 Judd Street, London WC1H 9NE

Tel: 020 7388 1266 Fax: 020 7388 2034 Helpline: 0845 766 9999

E-mail: helpline@rnib.org.uk Website: www.rnib.org.uk

RNID (Royal National Institute for Deaf and Hard of Hearing People)

19–23 Featherstone Street, London EC1Y 8SL

Tel: 0808 808 0123 Fax: 020 7296 8199 Textphone: 0808 808 9000

E-mail: informationline@rnid.org.uk Website: www.rnid.org.uk

SCOPE

6 Market Road, London, N7 9PW

Cerebral Palsy Helpline 0808 800 3333

E-mail: cphelpline@scope.org.uk; information@scope.org.uk

Website: www.scope.org.uk

SENSE (for people who are deafblind or have associated disabilities)

11–13 Clifton Terrace, Finsbury Park, London N4 3SR

Tel: 020 7272 7774 Fax: 020 7272 6012 Textphone: 020 7272 9648

E-mail: enquiries@sense.org.uk

Website: www.sense.org.uk

Stirling Dementia Services Development Centre

University of Stirling, Stirling FK9 4LA

Tel: 01786 467740 Fax: 01786 466846

E-mail: mtm1@stirling.ac.uk

Website: www.stir.ac.uk/Departments/HumanSciences/AppSocSci/DS

The British Tinnitus Association

Ground Floor, Unit 5, Acorn Business Park, Woodseats Close, Sheffield S8 0TB

Tel: 0114 250 9933 or freephone 0800 018 0527 Fax: 0114 2587059

E-mail: info@tinnitus.org.uk Website: www.tinnitus.org.uk

The Relatives and Residents Association

5 Tavistock Place, London WC1H 9SN

Tel: 020 7692 4302 Fax: 020 7916 6093 Advice Line: 020 7916 6055

E-mail: relres@totalise.co.uk

The Sickle Cell Society

54 Station Road, Harlesden, London NW10 4UA

Tel: 020 8961 7795/4006 Fax: 020 8961 8346

E-mail: sickleinfo.line@btinternet.com Website: www.sicklecellsociety.org

The Stroke Association

Stroke House, Whitecross Street, London EC1 8JJ

Tel: 0207 566 0300 Fax: 0207 490 2686 Information Service: 0845 30 33 100

E-mail: info@stroke.org.uk Website: www.stroke.org.uk

Victim Support

Cranmer House, 39 Brixton Road, London SW9 6DZ

Tel: 020 7735 9166 Fax: 020 7582 5712

Voice UK

Room B11, The College Business Centre, Uttoxeter New Road, Derby DE22 3WZ

Tel: 01332 869311/2/4 Fax: 01332 869318 Helpline: 0870 013 3965

E-mail: voiceUK@clara.net

Website: www.voiceuk.clara.net

References

Action on Elder Abuse (1995) *Bulletin No 11*. London: AEA.

Action on Elder Abuse (April 2002) *Responding to Abuse in Residential and Day Care Settings* leaflet. London: AEA.

Alibhai-Brown, Y. (1998) *Caring for Ethnic Minority Elders*. London: Age Concern England.

Alzheimer's Society (June 2001) Information Sheet 400 *What is Dementia?* London: Alzheimer's Society.

Arnold, L. and Babiker, G. (1998) 'Counselling People Who Self-Injure.' In Z. Bear (ed) *Good Practice in Counselling People Who Have Been Abused*. London: Jessica Kingsley Publishers.

Arnold, L. and Magill, A. (1996) *Working with Self-Injury: A Practical Guide*. Bristol: The Basement Project.

Association of Directors of Social Services (1987) *Guidelines and Recommendations to Employers on Violence Against Employees in the Personal Social Services*. ADSS: Reading.

Baker, A.A. (1975) 'Granny Battering.' *Modern Geriatrics 5*, 8, 20–24.

Bornat, J. (ed) (1994) *Reminiscence Reviewed: Perspectives, Evaluations, Achievements*. Buckingham: Open University Press.

Braithwaite, R. (2001) *Managing Aggression*. London: Routledge.

Brearley, C.P. (1982a) *Risk and Ageing*. London: Routledge and Kegan Paul.

Brearley, C.P. (1982b) *Risk in Social Work*. London: Routledge and Kegan Paul.

British Dyslexia Association (April 2002) *What is Dyslexia?* AO1. Reading: British Dyslexia Association.

British Institute of Learning Disabilities (July 2001) Fact Sheet 1 *Learning Disability*. Kidderminster: BILD.

British Medical Association and Law Society (1995) *Assessment of Mental Capacity*. London: BMA and Law Society.

Burston, G.R. (1975) 'Granny Battering.' *British Medical Journal 3*, 592–3.

Burston, G.R. (1977) 'Do Your Elderly Patients Live in Fear of Being Battered?' *Modern Geriatrics 7*, 5, 54–55.

Burton-Jones, J. (2001) *Involving Relatives and Friends: A Good Practice Guide for Homes for Older People.* London: The Relatives and Residents Association.

Caldicott Committee (1997) *Report on the Review of Patient-Identifiable Information.* London: Department of Health.

Clarke, A. and Bright, L. (2002) *Showing Restraint: Challenging the Use of Restraint in Care Homes.* London: Counsel and Care.

Coleman, V., Regan, D. and Smith, J. (1999) *Who Care Plans.* London: Counsel and Care.

Compact Oxford English Dictionary (2000) Oxford: Oxford University Press.

Counsel and Care (1992) *What if They Hurt Themselves.* London: Counsel and Care.

Counsel and Care (1993) *The Right to Take Risks.* London: Counsel and Care.

Counsel and Care (1995) *Last Rights.* London: Counsel and Care.

Counsel and Care (2002) *Residents Taking Risks: Minimising the Use of Restraint – A Guide for Care Homes.* London: Counsel and Care.

Cruse Bereavement Care *Has Someone Died?* London: CRUSE.

Department of Health (1989) *Homes Are For Living In.* London: HMSO.

Department of Health (1991) *Care Management and Assessment: Practitioners' Guide.* London: HMSO.

Department of Health (1993) *No Longer Afraid: The Safeguard of Older People in Domestic Settings.* London: HMSO.

Department of Health (2000a) *No Secrets: Guidance on Developing and Implementing Multi-Agency Policies and Procedures to Protect Vulnerable Adults from Abuse.* London: HMSO.

Department of Health (2000b) *No Secrets: Guidance on Developing and Implementing Multi-Agency Policies and Procedures to Protect Vulnerable Adults from Abuse.* Health Service/Local Authority Circular HSC 2000/007. London: NHS Executive.

Department of Health (2000c) *We Don't Have To Take This* Resource Pack. London: Department of Health.

Department of Health (2001a) *A Safer Place: Combating Violence Against Social Care Staff.* London: Department of Health.

Department of Health (2001b) *National Service Framework for Older People.* London: Department of Health.

Department of Health (2002) *National Minimum Standards for Care Homes for Older People* 2nd edition. London: The Stationery Office.

Eastman, M. (1984) *Old Age Abuse.* London: Age Concern.

Emerson, E. (2001) *Challenging Behaviour: Analysis and Intervention in People with Severe Intellectual Disabilities.* 2nd Edition. Cambridge: Cambridge University Press.

Gibson, F. (1998) *Reminiscence and Recall.* 2nd Edition. London: Age Concern.

Gillies, C. and James, A. (1994) *Reminiscence Work with Old People.* London: Chapman and Hall.

Goldsmith, M. (1996) *Hearing the Voice of People with Dementia.* London: Jessica Kingsley Publishers.

Hawkins, P. and Shohet, R. (2000) *Supervision in the Helping Professions.* Buckingham: Open University Press.

Health and Safety Regulations Commission (1992) *The Management of Health and Safety at Work. Approved Code of Practice.* London: HMSO.

Henley, A. and Schott, J. (1999) *Culture, Religion and Patient Care in a Multi-Ethnic Society.* London: Age Concern England.

Heron, J. (1975) *Six Category Intervention Analysis.* Guildford: University of Surrey.

Hilton, C. and Hyder, M. (1998) *Getting to Grips with Punctuation and Grammar.* London: Letts Educational.

Holden, U. and Chapman, A. (1994) *'Wait A Minute!' – A Practice Guide on Challenging Behaviour and Aggression for Staff Working with Individuals Who Have Dementia.* Stirling: Dementia Services Development Centre.

Home Office (2001a) *Human Rights Act: An Introduction.* London: Home Office Communication Directorate.

Home Office (2001b) *Study Guide: Human Rights Act 1998.* London: Home Office Communication Directorate.

Honey, P. and Mumford, A. (2000a) *The Learning Styles Helper's Guide.* Maidenhead: Peter Honey Publications.

Honey, P. and Mumford, A. (2000b) *The Learning Styles Questionnaire (80-item version).* Maidenhead: Peter Honey Publications.

Hopkins, G. (1998a) *Plain English for Social Services: A Guide to Better Communication.* Lyme Regis: Russell House Publishing.

Hopkins, G. (1998b) *The Write Stuff: A Guide to Effective Writing in Social Care and Related Services.* Lyme Regis: Russell House Publishing.

Howard, H. (2000) *The Care Assistant's Handbook.* London: Age Concern England.

Hughes, A. (2001) 'The Role of the Registration and Inspection Officer.' In J. Pritchard (ed) *Good Practice with Vulnerable Adults.* London: Jessica Kingsley Publishers.

Hunt, L., Marshall, M. and Rowlings, C. (1997) *Past Trauma in Late Life.* London: Jessica Kingsley Publishers.

Jacobs, M. (1985) *Swift to Hear.* London: SPCK.

Kadushin, A. (1976) *Supervision in Social Work.* New York: Columbia University Press.

Kolb, D. (1984) *Experiential Learning.* Englewood Cliffs, NJ: Prentice-Hall.

Kubler-Ross, E. (1995) *On Death and Dying.* London: Routledge.

Lawson, J. (1996) 'A Framework for Risk Assessment and Management for Older People.' In H. Kemshall and J. Pritchard (eds) *Good Practice in Risk Assessment and Risk Management.* London: Jessica Kingsley Publishers.

Littlechild, R. (1996) 'Risk and Older People.' In H. Kemshall and J. Pritchard (eds) *Good Practice in Risk Assessment and Risk Management.* London: Jessica Kingsley Publishers.

Lord Chancellor's Department (1997) *Who Decides?:Making Decisions on Behalf of Mentally Incapacitated Adults.* London: The Stationery Office.

Lord Chancellor's Department (1999) *Making Decisions: The Government's Proposals for Making Decisions on Behalf of Mentally Incapacitated Adults.* London: The Stationery Office.

Lord Chancellor's Department (2002) *Making Decisions: Helping People Who Have Difficulty Deciding for Themselves.* Consultation Paper CP 05/2002. London: The Lord Chancellor's Department.

Mallinson, I. (1995) *Keyworking in Social Care: A Structured Approach to Provision.* London: Whiting and Birch.

Mallinson, I. (1996) *Care Planning in Residential Care for Older People in Scotland.* Aldershot: Avebury.

Mandelstam, M. (1998) *An A–Z of Community Care Law.* London: Jessica Kingsley Publishers.

MIND (2001) *Understanding Mental Illness* booklet. London: MIND.

Morrison, T. (2001) *Staff Supervision in Social Care.* Brighton: Pavilion Publishing.

Murphy, C.J. (1994) *'It Started with a Sea-Shell': Life Story Work and People with Dementia.* Stirling: Dementia Services Development Centre.

Neuberger, J. (1994) *Caring for Dying People of Different Faiths.* London: Mosby.

Parkes, C.M. and Markus, A. (1998) *Coping with Loss.* London: BMJ Books.

Payne, C. and Scott, T. (1985) *Developing Supervision of Teams in Field and Residential Social Work.* Parts 1 and 2. London: National Institute for Social Work.

Population Trends (Summer 1999) *96.*

Population Trends (Autumn 2001) *105.*

Pritchard, J. (ed) (1995) *Good Practice in Supervision.* London: Jessica Kingsley Publishers.

Pritchard, J. (1996) *Working with Elder Abuse: A Training Manual for Home Care, Residential and Day Care Staff.* London: Jessica Kingsley Publishers.

Pritchard, J. (1997) 'Vulnerable People Taking Risks: Older People and Residential Care.' In H. Kemshall and J. Pritchard (eds) *Good Practice in Risk Assessment and Risk Management 2: Protection, Rights and Responsibilities.* London: Jessica Kingsley Publishers.

Pritchard, J. (2000) *The Needs of Older Women: Services for Victims of Elder Abuse and Other Abuse.* Bristol: The Policy Press.

Pritchard, J. (2001a) *Becoming a Trainer in Adult Abuse Work.* London: Jessica Kingsley Publishers.

Pritchard, J. (ed) (2001b) *Good Practice with Vulnerable Adults.* London: Jessica Kingsley Publishers.

Pritchard, J. (2001c) *Male Victims of Elder Abuse: Their Experiences and Needs.* London: Jessica Kingsley Publishers.

Richards, M. and Payne, C. (1990) *Staff Supervision in Child Protection Work.* London: National Institute of Social Work.

Rochdale Metropolitan Borough Council (2000) *Risk Assessment and Risk Management.* Rochdale: Rochdale Social Services Department.

Scrutton, S. (1995) *Bereavement and Grief: Supporting Older People Through Loss.* London: Edward Arnold.

Sherman, B. (1999) *Sex, Intimacy and Aged Care*. London: Jessica Kingsley Publishers.

Smith, P. (1998) *Death and Dying in a Nursing Home*. Norwich: Social Work Monographs.

The Samaritans (April 2002) Information taken from: www.samaritans.org.uk/know/statistics_suicide.html

Thomas, M. and Pierson, J. (1995) *Dictionary of Social Work*. London: Collins Educational.

Thompson, N. (2002) *Loss and Grief: A Guide for Human Services Practitioners*. Basingstoke: Palgrave.

Training Organisation for the Personal Social Services (2001) *The First Six Months: A Registered Manager's Guide to Induction and Foundation Standards*. Leeds: TOPSS.

United Kingdom Central Council for Nursing, Midwifery and Health Visiting (1999) *Practitioner–Client Relationships and the Prevention of Abuse*. London: UKCC.

Subject Index

Name Index